D0865492

FIVA

An Adventure That Went Wrong

Gordon Stainforth

GOLDEN ARROW BOOKS

First published in Great Britain in 2012 by
Golden Arrow Books
Wesleyan House, West End, Brassington,
Derbyshire DE4 4HL
www.goldenarrowbooks.co.uk

Copyright © Gordon Stainforth 2012

Gordon Stainforth has asserted his rights under the Copyright,
Designs and Patents Act 1988 to be identified as author of this work.

"The Son Of Hickory Holler's Tramp"
Written by Dallas Frazier
©1967 Sony/ATV Music Publishing LLC. All rights administered by
Sony/ATV Music Publishing LLC
All rights reserved. Used by permission

Words from "Runaway" used with kind permission of
Del Shannon Enterprises, Inc.

A CIP catalogue record for this book
is available from the British Library

ISBN 978-0-9570543-0-1

*All rights reserved. No part of this publication may be reproduced, transmitted,
or stored in a retrieval system, in any form or by any means, without written
permission from the publisher except in the case of brief quotations embedded in
critical articles or reviews*

Printed and bound by CPI Group (UK) Ltd, Croydon, CR0 4YY

To our father
Peter Stainforth
who gave us so much rope

John and Gordon about to leave their home in Hertfordshire for Norway on June 27, 1969
Photo: Peter Stainforth

CONTENTS

LIST OF ILLUSTRATIONS

(All photographs, unless otherwise credited, by John Stainforth)

PREFACE

I have known all my adult life that one day I would write a book about the near-death experience I had in 1969 with my twin brother on Store Trolltind, the highest mountain in the Romsdal region of Norway. The name of the route, the four-letter word 'Fiva' (pronounced 'Fever'), has remained seared into my memory for all time like the secret code for a necessary rite of passage.

So when, in May 2009, my brother casually suggested that it would be fun to go on a 40th anniversary return trip to Romsdal, I jumped at the idea. We realised that if we got our act together we could be there in early July, in the very week of the anniversary.

Thus, forty years to the very day that we had become ensnared on the climb, we found ourselves peering over the mile-high abyss to gaze down on it once more. It did not disappoint: if anything it seemed more alien than ever. A few days later, we made the long and easy ascent of Nordre Trolltind, a northern subsidiary summit of Store Trolltind, in the hope of being able to look directly at the top half of the route. We had been told that the viewpoint was stupendous, but sadly, by the time we reached the top, we were in cloud. We waited several hours when, at last, with splendid theatricality, the savage pointed summit of Store Trolltind pierced the boiling cloud hundreds of feet above our heads, and a few minutes later the whole of the Troll Wall, the highest vertical rockwall in Europe, emerged directly opposite us. Finally, the cloud in the deep gully below the summit of Store Trolltind cleared and we were looking with a kind of God's-eye view at the top two thousand feet of the Fiva Route, about a quarter of a mile away. We just stood and gaped at its inhospitality, feeling very fortunate to have had such interesting lives, which could so easily have been brought to an abrupt end in that grim chasm forty years before.

For the next four months, John and I entered into an intensive period of research, piecing together all the details of the climb – from our own logbook accounts and rather differing memories of it – but helped enormously by all the new photographs we had taken. We drew diagrams, had endless debates, and gradually worked out the exact time scenario virtually to the nearest five minutes.

After several false starts – such is often the way with writing – I decided to tell the whole story in the first-person present tense. This was a great challenge, in that I had to put myself back into the mountaineering boots of a 19-year-old with a very limited perspective on life and a rather exaggerated assessment of his climbing ability. All my youthful shortcomings and misconceptions had to be reproduced. For example, we had unjustly blamed the guidebook for many of our problems, when really they were the result of our total inexperience of climbing big mountain routes with typically minimal descriptions. The guidebook we used was published by the Rimmon Mountaineering Club in 1966 at the request of their sponsors to promote climbing in Norway after their successful Troll Wall climb. Much of it was based on previous climbers' notes, and it was superseded within a year of our Fiva epic by a carefully revised edition, which included a corrected description of the Fiva Route. I'm happy to say that Tony Howard has taken my teenage comments about his earlier edition in good heart; and I should add that his latest version, published in 2005, remains indispensable to any English-speaking climber visiting the area (see Further Reading on p.211 for details).

Likewise, the tough fingerless 'Millar mitts' we used, made by a company in Nottingham that has sadly long since gone out of business, were never intended to be used as 'belay gloves', and so my youthful assessment of them is thoroughly misleading. I should also point out that a modern Space Blanket bears little resemblance to the one we used in 1969, and is strongly recommended as a piece of emergency equipment.

Finally, I must thank all those who have helped bring this

book to fruition. First, those who read the final draft and made helpful comments: Chris Bonington, Steve Dean, Peter Gillman, Tony Howard, Charles Masefield, Hilary and Kevin McKay, Jenny Trigona, and Stephen Venables. Then Nils-Inge Salen and Ragnhild Hjelmstad for their help at Trollstigen Resort, our base on our 2009 return trip; Bill and Elizabeth Bromley-Davenport for their hospitality at Fiva Farm in 2009; Brian Capper and Hugh Tassell for their recollections of our arrival back at Fiva Farm in 1969; Nicholas Ashton for providing an English translation of Eirik Heen's 1932 account of the first ascent of the Fiva Route; Tony Howard for permission to reproduce three pages of his 1966 interim guide; Chris Fitzhugh for his unfailing belief in me; my agent, John Parker, for his encouragement and advice over many years; and, last but not least, the two 'other halves' in my life, Freda Raphael, who has been my emotional bedrock, and John for all his painstaking help with the research and editing, and of course his role in the original adventure.

Gordon Stainforth
Belper, October 2011

Gordon cooking supper at our tent near Fiva Farm on Saturday, July 5 1969

I

SUNDAY

It's the big moment, the moment of no return. Deep down, we know it's mad, but we're doing it anyway. It's T-minus one minute to blast off, and I'm crouched in a sombre clearing in the woods, as if in some gigantic upscaled cathedral, with mile-high rock walls towering above me while cloud wreathes in slow motion about its great buttresses, turrets and spires.

My twin brother, John – nineteen years old – his climbing sack already clamped to his back, watches silently as I fumble with a scrap of paper pressed against the guidebook on my knee, having trouble getting my biro to write …

We're like the last two miniscule representatives of humanity standing in the bowels of a great prehistoric canyon on a cold damp midsummer Sunday morning in Norway. That's unlike any other Sunday morning we've ever experienced.

There's no sound at all, apart from an indeterminate burble of running water and the hiss of a thousand waterfalls. The whole ancient mountain landscape is steaming, as if the rock itself were breathing and coming to life, exhaling the smoke of an age-old energy at the dawn of yet another day, in yet another year, in yet another millennium …

And now the ink is coming. It's the critical moment in a special rite that has all the feeling of a pivotal moment in life. We've discussed the exact wording so carefully in the last few minutes that John might as well be dictating it to me without even opening his mouth.

I write in large capital letters:

FIVA ROUTE

I go over it again because the biro is starting to write better, and then underscore it with as confident a line as I can muster. Then below I add, very neatly centred,

BACK SUNDAY NIGHT
OR LATEST
MONDAY MORNING

Just nine words. How irrevocably one's fate can be sealed by just a few simple words.

"OK?" I say.

"Yes," says John.

I impale the piece of paper neatly and decisively on the metal spike at the apex of our oddly lopsided "Good Companion" tent – a faded orange wigwam that vaguely resembles a mountain peak in miniature.

There's no turning back now. We're totally committed. T-minus 10 seconds and counting.

We're leaving the note mostly for the benefit of the rest of our party, who'll be arriving in a day or two. We've left them in the Jotunheim, a mountain range a hundred miles to the south, and have moved on here while the weather is bad because, really, Romsdal is the place where it's all at now, and we know there'll be a whole lot more English climbers arriving in the next few days. We're just a bit ahead of the game, that's all. You know – Apollo 11 is still on the launch pad at Cape Kennedy, waiting to go to the Moon, and we've blasted off already.

We're grown up now, we've left school, and we're needing *the big adventure*. Any of our friends will tell you that we've really got the climbing fever. *OK?* We've climbed a couple of quite big mountains in the Alps with guides, and we've done dozens of rock climbs (last year) in North Wales, and now we're going to tackle the biggest rock wall in Europe – *OK?*

Yes, Romsdal really is now at the forefront of "Big Wall Climbing" in Europe, and these are truly revolutionary times, in climbing as elsewhere.

"Ve go, yah!" John declares, imitating Heinrich Taugwalder, our Swiss guide on our first big Alpine climb.

I heave my sack onto my back. It's surprisingly heavy because, although we've made sure we're not taking one ounce more gear than we need, I lost the toss last night, so now I'm carrying the rope – a monstrous three-hundred-foot bundle of bright red and yellow nylon.

John gives a little smirk. "Don't do anything I wouldn't do!" – now he's cheekily imitating our grandmother as we left Knebworth railway station just ten days ago. And I smile with a naughty glow of schoolboy connivance. My God, Hertfordshire seems a long way away now! Knebworth's just so boring that everybody rightly calls it "Deadworth" – it's the very opposite of a happening place, about as far away as you can possibly imagine from anything connected with the pop scene, for example.

Now, dwarfed by an outrageous landscape of mountain superlatives, my heart is pounding with excitement, a strange mixture of fear and anticipation. Why did I say that what we're doing's mad? Because the climb we've chosen is so obviously out of condition, that's why! It's all much too wet, there's a lot of snow in the gullies, and the initial two thousand-foot slabs are glistening with water. And, although the weather's freshened up now, with the wind round to the north, the brooding mists don't look particularly promising. But we don't see it that way. We *won't* see it that way!

So we're off, without so much as a backward glance at our lonely little orange tent, our Cape Kennedy, as it drops away behind us. We head towards the trees at the back of the clearing where we know there's a small track. We checked it out last night when we went all the way up through the woods to make sure we wouldn't waste any time in the morning.

And no one could accuse us of that. We wanted to be off by four, but we've saved quarter of an hour by not even having any breakfast. We were going to have a hot drink, but John suddenly said, "Let's not waste time fiddling around with the Primus," and I wholeheartedly agreed. All the fiddle and fuss with meths and paraffin is the last thing you need before setting off on a serious climb. It was really totally unnecessary anyway because last night we each had double helpings of Vesta Beef Curry with Rice – actually, come to think of it, John had Chicken Chow Mein – and we even treated ourselves to some Cadbury's powdered potato. So now we're high on monosodium glutomate, and ready for anything. And *ahead of the game!*

While we were preparing supper two other English climbers passed us *en route* to the foot of the famous "Troll Pillar", which was first climbed by the legendary Norwegian, Arne Randers Heen, years ahead of its time, over ten years ago, back in 1958. (And, nearly thirty years before that, way back in 1931, Heen made the first ascent of the Fiva Route – pronounced "Fever" – that we're attempting now, which was positively futuristic for its date. Indeed, these were the only two routes to breach the whole of the Romsdal side of the Trolltindane massif until the Troll Wall itself was first climbed just four years ago.)

So, because they looked very experienced, we asked them for some tips on the Fiva Route. One of them – Tony, I think his name was – made very light of it; and when we asked him what sort of food we should take, he just laughed and said, "Oh, you'll be alright with a couple of Mars Bars on that!" Well, we haven't got any Mars Bars, but we have got a couple of bars of Cadbury's Fruit and Nut, which is even better, and we've got three cheese sandwiches. (We would have made four but we ran out of bread.) Oh, and a spare lump of cheese.

4.00 am

Everything in the woods is damp and dripping. It's a chaotic, ramshackle entanglement of ancient birch, littered with boulders and rocks of all sizes that are matted with moss and criss-crossed with old roots and rotten branches that shower droplets on us as we push the smaller ones out of the way. We pick our route carefully, being sure to remain on the faint muddy footpath that could easily be mistaken for an animal track.

It's quite a thought just how many of the best rock climbers in Europe – well, at least from Scandanavia, Britain and France – must have been along this faint elitist path over the last three or four years. Now that we've done our training, it's our turn to join the elite because we're really quite experienced now. Particularly last year, which we'll always call our great "summer of '68", when we broke into the Very Severe and Hard Very Severe grades for the first time. And this year we've been out at every possible opportunity. I've even been on a snow and ice climbing course in Glencoe – so technically, really, we can cope with anything.

We've also got all the latest gear: seven chrome-moly steel pegs of different sizes, including two "knifeblades" for the thinnest cracks, and eight "nuts" – small metal wedges of different shapes and sizes, up to about two inches wide for larger cracks, each threaded on its own nylon sling. We've also got five separate nylon slings, each with its own karabiner – or "krab" (the climbers' term for a metal snaplink). And we're even taking an ice axe with us – though Tony Howard in the guidebook says it's not necessary – because we can see there's quite a lot of snow up there. So we've thought of every eventuality, really.

Oh, and the "Space Blanket"! I must tell you about this fabulous new gismo called a "Space Blanket". It's a huge sheet of very thin Mylar plastic with a silver metallic coating on one side. It's about six feet square, big enough to cover two people, yet it packs down into this minute little silver packet about the size of a Mars Bar. It's not only completely waterproof, it also reflects back over ninety per cent of your body heat. And the silver foil means it'll also pick up searchlight beams … It's a real breakthrough in safety – one of the great new spin-offs of the Space Age. As used by NASA. So we're right in there and part of it; and we're going on our own Space Odyssey now, yeah!

We're doing the Fiva Route because Tony Willmott at the YHA shop in London has told us "it's a cracking route … You really must do it! The top of it's this amazing two-thousand-foot chimney-gully. It's really epic, a real classic."

Our plan is, if the Fiva goes well, we're then going to do the "Troll Pillar".

We've come out of the woods now, into the open, and the monstrous mile-high dinosaur of the Trolltindane is standing over us exuding superiority – its colossal limbs and wet flanks steaming in the dawn. We have to creep up on this monster very carefully if we are going to catch it unawares and get safely established among the huge wrinkles of its ancient hide, cracked and fissured with the age of aeons. Just what it's going to be like up there has an extreme fascination for us that pulls us, lures us on. But it's very daunting, too. The two-thousand-foot introductory slabs seem to have grown enormously as we've approached, and look smoother than ever. The lowest part is like a huge swollen tongue sweeping down to engulf us, curling over at the end in a great bulging wave of overhangs. A bit like the terrible oxtail soup they used to give us at Prep School, which had a skin on it so thick that you could flip the bowl almost on end, and the soup would bulge right out without any risk of the skin breaking.

Fortunately, just above this initial rock bulge, an enormous rake cuts diagonally across the introductory slabs for their full height, and that's the way our route goes. But it doesn't look at all inviting because it's obviously very vegetated. And the wall above it is absolutely awesome, rearing up for over four thousand feet to the near vertical. I've never seen anything remotely like it before, or remotely as repulsive.

But our hearts are set now and we mustn't waver for a moment. Best not even to look up at it. Best just to keep our heads to the ground, concentrating on the steep grass slope in front of us. But even that's not so encouraging, because I can't help noticing a profusion of disturbingly fresh looking, sharp-edged rock fragments scattered all around us like scales off the dinosaur's back. But, then, I suppose it's only to be expected below a face of this size. It's really mere dust in relation to the mountain. *Hey man, dinosaur's dandruff!*

God, this slope is hot work! I'm already getting overheated in my Norwegian sweater, and my Viyella shirt is soaked with perspiration. The three-hundred-foot rope feels very heavy this morning (yes, I've definitely drawn the short straw on this one), and my legs are feeling quite tired even before we've set foot on the climb.

4.30 am

We're standing below a surprisingly clean slab of rough greyish yellow rock that's remarkably reminiscent of the start of the Idwal Slabs in Snowdonia. Because of the way the crag curls over at the bottom, we can't see much above. We might as well be at the foot of a Welsh rock climb – except this one goes on for over six thousand feet …

Neither of us is saying anything. We're both getting our gear out of our sacks for the start of the first great ritual: the donning of the hemp waistlines. The hemp is a nominal quarter of an inch in diameter, almost silky to the touch, and has a very distinctive, pungent almondy smell that has over the last three years already become wonderful to us as a harbinger of outrageous adventures (I nearly said outrageous fortune!) The smell is so evocative that you can't hold the hemp to your nose without it conjuring up epic visions of heroic deeds.

I love this ritual that marks the start of a step into a new dimension, when we leave *terra cognita* behind, and put space below our feet. We each find the centre point of our hemp lines, and then wind them quite tightly around our waists, all twenty-four feet of them, round and round, our hands crossing over methodically in front of us seven times – girding our loins as it were – until at last we reach the neatly whipped ends, and tie them together with a simple reef knot. Then we ease open the strands of the rope with our thumbs, and tuck the ends into the lay of the rope so that they are tidily stashed out of the way. Then we clip our matt-black steel Hiatt D-screw karabiners around all the strands of hemp rope so that we're now wearing our very own custom-made climbing belts, all ready for action.

Since John's leading off, he starts clipping the various "nuts" into his waistline and puts the sling with the seven heavy pegs on it over one shoulder. I'm uncoiling the rope – it's already been coiled doubled – and hand John his two ends, for this type of rope is always used doubled, giving us a maximum length of a hundred and fifty feet for each pitch. It's nearly brand new; we only got it three weeks ago, and have used it just once on the limestone crag of Stoney Middleton in Derbyshire. Again, how far away that seems now!

I tie a figure-of-eight knot in the rope and clip the loop into my waist karabiner. Ready to go? Not quite. One more thing. My peg hammer. I slip it into the special sleeve on the right side of my breeches, and clip its safety line into my waist krab.

I suddenly realize that I've got quite cold since we've stopped. The northerly breeze has definitely freshened. Since I'm going to be standing at the bottom belaying John while he leads the first pitch, I'm going to get frozen.

"I'm going to put my anorak on," I tell him.

John looks at the clouds. "Actually, I'm going to do the same. I think the wind's got up, and I'd rather be a bit too hot than too cold."

It's about the first thing we've said for about five minutes.

We're already wearing our big red Compton helmets in case of any rock fall, so now we take them off and put our anoraks on over our sweaters. Then we put our helmets on again.

Our anoraks are absolutely new for this trip. John's is navy blue and mine is orange, not really through choice but because those were the only colours we could get in our sizes. They have a lovely new smell of "ventile" cotton, and are very comfortable; but it's certainly an unusual amount to be wearing on a rock climb.

At last we're nearly ready. John has sat down on a small boulder to tighten his laces on his brand new big, brown Galibier Super Gratton leather boots. My nice black Terray Fitzroys are still very tight, though they have become a bit more comfortable since I've been wearing them in the Jotunheim.

I'm putting a nut in a good crack in the big boulder beside me, because it's good practice to attach yourself to the mountain even at the foot of a climb in case the leader comes off and goes shooting off down the steep slope below. The nut that fits is my favourite, called a "MOAC", which stands for Mountain Activities, the people who make it.

Mountain activities! You can say that again!

"Watch me," John says, and without further ado he sets off up the slab with all the air of one who has done the climb a thousand times before.

"What's the rock like?" I ask. It's the first big question of course. This is where theory stops and we come up against raw reality. The proof is always in the pudding.

"It's very good – it's quite rough … a bit rougher than I was expecting. Nice gneiss !" It's an old joke, but he means it.

A bit higher up: "Umm … There's not much protection …" (He means cracks or spikes for attaching any running belays, or "runners", to.) "Well, nothing, actually! The rock's very blind – but it's very easy."

So, at first slowly and methodically, but getting steadily faster, John makes his way upwards, the heels of his boots silhouetted against the sky. To use our space metaphor, you could say that what he's doing now is putting behind him the pull of earth's gravity.

This ramp is totally unlike anywhere I've ever been in my life. I've certainly never been in an environment that's made me feel so small, or time so irrelevant. It's as if we've been transported back into some alien, prehistoric world. Our surroundings are so ginormous that we've been reduced to two tiny little ants making our way diagonally leftwards up an immense hanging garden of decaying, overgrown ledges that harbour odd shrubs of indeterminate species. It really wouldn't surprise me if at any moment we're bombed by angry pterodactyls or, on rounding a corner, we find a triceratops grazing on a grassy terrace.

Well over two hours ago, after just three introductory pitches up nice easy ("easy gneiss"!) slabs, the climbing became so straightforward that we unroped – and now John's having to carry it in a great three-hundred-foot shank lashed to the back of his sack. We've also taken off our anoraks because, while we were on the slabs the sun came out for a while, and we were definitely overheating. Despite the cold wind and the fact that we're now just climbing in our sweaters, it's really hot work toiling up these endless slabs and grass rakes. But we've been going so fast, unroped, that it feels as if we've gone up in an aeroplane. The valley floor, with the minute orange speck of our tent in the clearing in the woods below, is now laid out behind us like a map. And, all the time, rising straight ahead of us, beyond the shoulder at the top of the slabs, is the great five-thousand-foot vertical rock curtain of the Troll Wall. Even though it's still over half a mile away, it's grown so enormous that it's difficult to comprehend.

Although the climbing's very easy, it's all rather insecure. It's what we call "grotty" in climbing parlance (derived perhaps from grottoes, or the grotesque), but not "manky" – quite. That's something a lot worse, usually implying green slime. This is just a bit wet, or at least the grass is. Which means it's really quite treacherous, in that a single slip would send you tumbling two thousand feet to the bottom. No, you wouldn't want to slip here.

I can't help reflecting just how extraordinary it is that our father – yes, as twins we always say it like that, "Our Father", even though he has his feet very firmly on the ground and not in heaven – has encouraged us to do something as absurdly dangerous as mountaineering. Especially in the context of our mother's recent death of cancer, an indelible tragedy that has blown a huge hole in our family. Yet Dad, far from being averse to our climbing, has actively supported and encouraged us every inch of the way. It's clearly very much in his nature to do so. The War years for him, when he became a paratrooper, were a huge adventure. As a Royal Engineer, he volunteered to join a new company called the "Airborne Forces" that he'd seen advertised on a noticeboard before he even knew what it was – mostly because he wanted to avoid being put into the Chemical Warfare Unit – and found himself being sent on daring missions to North Africa, Tunisia and Italy, before being shot through the lung and taken prisoner at the catastrophic débâcle of the Battle of Arnhem. And, although he'd never been up a serious mountain before, he climbed the Matterhorn with our Aunt Hazel three years ago, when he took us all out to Zermatt to recuperate after our mother's death.

It was in Zermatt that we really got the climbing fever. Before we went, we read Edward Whymper's classic book *Scrambles Amongst the Alps*, all about his attempts and eventual success on the Matterhorn, and when we got there we took to climbing like ducks to water – well, marmots to rock, really.

So well did that first Alpine holiday go, and so keen were we when we got home, that Dad paid for us to go on a Mountaineering Association "Beginner's Rock Climbing" course in North Wales the following year, and then the three of us went back to Zermatt for the second year running. We climbed all over the Riffelhorn as a training peak, and this was where John and I did our first leading. We really wanted to do the Matterhorn above all else, but the Zermatt guides decreed against it because they had a strict rule that you had to be over eighteen, and we were still only seventeen. But it was agreed that we could do the slightly smaller Zinal Rothorn, a superb very pointed peak of thirteen thousand eight hundred and something feet. And who should we have as our guide but Heinrich Taugwalder, the great-great-grandson of Old Peter Taugwalder, who'd been on the ill-fated first ascent of the Matterhorn with Whymper in 1865?

Our ascent of the Zinal Rothorn went fantastically well, fantastical being the appropriate word, because it took us into a completely new, magic realm high above the clouds that we'd never experienced before. John and I literally scampered up it – Heinrich said we were like chamois, though he pointed out that we weren't nearly as nimble on the descent. When we got back to Zermatt, we all went for a celebratory meal at the famous Monte Rosa Hotel, which had been the virtual summer home of the London-based Alpine Club in the 1860s. When it came to settling the bill for the climb with the lovely old guide Emil Perren, who'd arranged the whole thing, Dad looked at it for a moment with puzzlement. "But this can't be right, Emil. It's not nearly enough …" And Emil said, with a little quizzical smile: "They are *twins* – two for the price of one!" It was a supremely touching moment, because Emil had known all about our mother's tragic death, and why we had come to Zermatt in the first place.

Our climbing then went from strength to strength. From the autumn of 1967, we climbed every single Sunday at Harrison's Rocks in Kent, which was within cycling distance of our school in Tonbridge – quite soon reaching the "dizzying heights" of the grade of 5c, represented by such famous gymnastic challenges as "The Niblick" and "Slim Finger Crack". Then came our great "summer of '68" – that great year in which students "were revolting", as Dad likes to put it – when we left school and spent the whole of August in Snowdonia, being blessed with not a single drop of rain, and climbing over seventy famous rock climbs, finishing the holiday on such hoary old Hard Very Severe classics as "Spectre" and "Kaisergebirge Wall" in the Llanberis Pass.

John and I form a really great climbing team. Rather unsurprisingly for twins, we're of a very similar ability, though John always seems to have a slight edge on me technically. There have been a couple of occasions when he's backed off a crux, and I've taken over, but mostly it's the other way round. Being twins makes for fantastic teamwork, and now we have an unshakeable rule that we always do alternate leads, come what may – whatever the nature of the challenge. There's remarkably little communication between us when we're climbing unless we're finding it unusually difficult, or can't find the route. I suppose you could say we climb with a kind of telepathy, sometimes just feeling what the other is thinking by the way the rope moves.

Looking down at John now, about twenty feet below me, I see that his face is pouring with sweat. He looks really weighed down by the three hundred feet of rope on the back of his sack. Having that extra weight makes climbing very awkward too, as it tends to throw you off balance. I don't envy him one little bit. So I very nobly offer to take it from him.

"No," John snaps, "I'm fine!" He knows, of course, that it's my turn to lead the next pitch, however nasty it may be. So what he really means is: "Oh no, mate, we don't break the sequence of the alternate leads!"

It's now become so dark and gloomy that we can hardly see the grass we're climbing, making this primeval landscape more forbidding than ever. It's not the sort of place any sane person would want to visit unless there was some desperately good reason to do so. The huge sloping grass field we are on is like an enormous thatched roof of thick wet grass set at an angle of about thirty degrees. We're just wading up through it, heaving on handfuls of grass, and our needlecord breeches are already saturated.

Some things we're finding very helpful now are our "rainstormproof" Millar mitts. These are very tough (and expensive – nineteen shillings a pair!) fingerless gloves that are meant for climbing wet rock, but we're finding them very useful for climbing this wet grass because of their fantastic grip. Advertisements for them proclaim: "as used on the Rimmon Route – with unique Slip-resisting Palm" – the Rimmon Route being in fact another name for the Troll Wall, because the first ascent in 1965 was made by the

Rimmon Mountaineering Club from the north Peak District, which included Tony Howard, the chap who's written our guidebook. The gloves certainly feel very "at home" here and their grip on this wet grass suggests that they're also going to work well as belay gloves, particularly when the rope gets wet. I've got a feeling that they're going to prove very useful higher on the route.

I'm humming to keep up my spirits as I haul my way up the interminable grass. On the ferry over from Newcastle to Bergen last week the band played almost nothing else but the Beatles' *Ob-La-Di, Ob-La-Da* and *Hey Jude,* and something with a name like *"Henry Harlot's Tramp"*; and now I can't get that tune out of my head.

> *Oh, the path was deep and wide*
> *From footsteps leading to our cabin …*
> *Each and every day …* (I can't remember the words)
> *… And late at night, a hand would knock,*
> *And there would stand a stranger –*
> *Yes, I'm the son of Henry Harlot's tramp!*

John – just in front of me now – hears me singing breathlessly and says: "You know, I can't get that bloody thing out of my head either! – Something about 'Mama's chicken dumplings'! Very weird!"

We lapse into silence. What a strange pilgrimage this is that we're embarked upon!

8.40 am

At last we come out onto a huge grassy shoulder at the top of the ramp, with a vertical wall on the far side plunging over two thousand feet to the screes. Directly facing us, blotting out the sky, is the great grey vertical sheet of the Troll Wall, a mile wide and a mile high, like an enormous defensive barricade fringed along its top with ferocious spikes to keep out any intruders, and completely blocking out any kind of mountain vista, or anything normal at all. I've been up to the start of the great four-thousand-foot Hörnli

ridge of the Matterhorn, but I've never seen anything remotely as impressive as this vast curtain of rock.

No language can adequately convey the truly outlandish nature of a mountain feature as gross and as savage as the Troll Wall. The problem with using the tired old metaphor of a "curtain of rock" is that it implies that there might be something flimsy or even accommodating about it, when its overriding characteristic is its unyielding barbarity. If you were to make a scale model of it and run your hand over its apparently smooth surface you would cut yourself to shreds on its sharp edges and jagged overhangs.

Further round to the left there is, at least, a view of the huge U-shaped valley of Romsdal. I'm sure that, apart from the faint lines of the road and railway, it would have looked exactly the same from this viewpoint five or six thousand years ago. At this time in the morning there is no sign of life at all. I can't even see our tent now in the deep gloom of the woods below. I can only guess approximately where it is, and this makes me feel more cut off from reality than ever as I break myself four squares of chocolate and have some water.

I look at my watch. It's twenty to nine. We've been on the damp flanks of this dinosaur for nearly *four hours*, even though we've been climbing very fast. Just where has the time gone? It seems that, with the enormously increased length of day in this land of the "Midnight Sun", time simply goes faster. Or is it that we've become smaller?

Despite our daunting surroundings, John's in a very good mood. Verging on the euphoric. "We're way up on schedule," he declares, sipping some water. "Our performance so far shows that we've got this baby licked!" (He's developed a penchant of late for groovy American expressions.) "At this rate we'll be at the top in another four to six hours!" He takes another sip of water.

Well, I suppose he's basing his calculation on the guidebook time for the whole route of eight to twelve hours, and I suppose that, even if we go very slowly and take twelve hours, we'll still get to the top about three this afternoon, and so we'll be at Stegfoss by about six at the latest. So we should certainly be back at our tent comfortably in time for supper. We'll have a really big celebration if the others have turned up from the Jotunheim …

But the truth is we haven't even started the *real* climbing yet.

John's worrying now about where the route goes, and this sudden sense of uncertainty is exacerbated by an unwelcome touch of drizzle. The only way we can go, we decide, is up the broad ridge of the shoulder directly above us. No doubt, in a minute, all will be revealed.

"God almighty!"

We've followed an obvious grass ledge leftwards below a steep buttress at the top of the shoulder, and now the upper half of our route is revealed in all its glory or, rather, all its stark horror, for the first time. If the introductory slabs seemed unwelcoming, they were nothing compared with this. Many climbs look friendlier when you get up close to them, but this looks about a thousand times worse.

Directly in front of us hangs the huge couloir of our route, with the great black pillar of Brudgommen on its left and the sheer south-west wall of Store Trolltind on its right, giving the impression of a gigantic gloomy barbican, with mist wreathing around its turrets. Everything looks very cold and damp, blackened with water streaks, and there's a lot more snow than we were expecting. It's all very gothic in style, utterly forbidding, and pregnant with hidden threats of all kinds.

I've learnt all about this kind of thing at school, of course. It's what Edmund Burke called "the Sublime", which means the very opposite of what it sounds like. It's got nothing to do with beauty, but is all about something that's awesome and thrilling at the same time. Well, this is so thrilling it's *shock horror!* Burke says that something's "sublime" if it's so huge and astonishing that it "completely fills the mind, so that it cannot entertain anything else". Well, that's certainly true of what we're looking at now. Gustav Doré I'm sure would have been in his element up here, sitting on this shoulder "on the edge of a great steep", making preliminary sketches for engravings of Dante's Inferno. Though Dante's famous opening words wouldn't be quite right here, of course. It isn't so much a case of "abandon all hope all ye who enter here" as abandon all sanity.

Just what have we got ourselves into?

John has pulled a very long face, pursing his lips, with his lower lip sticking right out. He reminds me a little bit of Les Dawson. Which gives me a chance to lighten the tone. I chuckle:

"Actually, John, it reminds me a bit of Les Dawson's 'fairytale honeymoon'."

"What's that?"

"Don't you remember? 'I've just been on this fairytale honeymoon …' 'Oh, and what was it like?' '… *Grim*'!"

This cheers John up a lot. He giggles, then says: "Well, it's certainly a bit bigger than Cloggy! Anyhow, we'd better stop staring at it, and get on with it!" (Cloggy is the climbers' nickname for Clogwyn d'ur Arddu, a cliff in Snowdonia, one of the largest crags in Britain south of the Scottish border.)

Straightaway, it seems, we are faced with a somewhat daunting "entrance exam". A kind of initiation ceremony. Above us, poised precariously above a steep barrier of smooth wet slabs, hangs the enormous snout of the central snowfield, forming an overhanging wall of snow. But, between us and the slabs, there is a totally unexpected ravine of unfathomable depth, that's not even mentioned in the guidebook – it just talks about going up the introductory rake "to a snow patch at the foot of the gully" – and we've obviously somehow got to get round this ravine to regain our route. On the opposite side, only about forty feet away from us, a broken ledge line leads across to a small snow patch beside the slabs. It looks very loose and unpleasant, but it's the only obvious way. What's more, it's my turn to lead.

It's a lot colder here beside the ravine, so we put our anoraks on again. John sets up a belay – placing a sling round a large boulder – while I "gear up", putting the bandolier of steel pegs round my neck, and clipping various nuts into my waistband. Then I carefully slot my ice axe into my rucksack shoulder strap because I'll need it to cross the snow patch.

"Now for something altogether different!" I announce portentously once I'm ready, quoting the words of the French guide Michel Croz to Edward Whymper on the first ascent of the Matterhorn. That John gets the reference he signifies with a curt little nod; but his look says, "Get on with it – stop farting about!"

The drizzle has stopped, but as I move into the confines of the dank, bottomless ravine, there's a nasty cold updraught. The change of mood is, well, quite chilling.

John falls silent as I edge my way carefully along a line of rotten ledges leading towards the back of the narrow zawn – testing each hold, rather as if I were moving along a cluttered mantelpiece of fragile ornaments.

"What's it like?" John asks. I wish he hadn't.

"Pretty horrible; but OK if you take it carefully … I'll put on lots of runners … It's not technically hard." I give him a kind of running commentary to reassure him, making it sound as matter-of-fact as possible, but mostly to boost my own confidence.

The back of the ravine is very rotten and gritty, but as soon as I step across it I find myself on much sounder rock on the far side. I drape a nylon tape sling around a solid spike as a runner, clip the red rope to it, and feel a lot happier. Soon I'm back almost opposite John, only about twenty feet away, with the yellow rope hanging heavily across the ravine like a cable-car, tugging unnervingly at my waist and threatening to pluck me from my holds.

"It's OK!" I report breezily. "It's not nearly as bad as it looks!"

Because of the drag on the red rope, I need to find somewhere soon to belay, but the rock where I'm standing is all far too loose. Ahead, the traverse line is blocked by a bank of snow, but beyond it there appears to be a kind of alcove.

I carefully extract my ice axe from my rucksack strap. I last used it in Glencoe in March, but since then I've had it shortened, and the pick curved. When Tony Willmott at the YHA shop in London recommended that we do the Fiva Route, one of the first things he advised was that we have our ice axes shortened. So the wooden shaft is now just fourteen inches long – so short that it scarcely merits the term "ice axe" in the traditional sense of the word. And this is the very first time I've used it in its new incarnation.

The snow turns out to be the most peculiar stuff, very wet and sugary, but with a hard crust of ice that's peppered with pieces of black grit that have obviously been washed down the mountain, suggesting that it's melted a lot in the last few days and has now frozen over again.

I quickly cut some steps in the ice, whack the pick in as a handhold – hey, this new curved pick is really ace! – and step across. Repeating the process, I'm across the snow slope in a couple of minutes, and find myself in a deep gravelly slot where the snow has melted away from the rock. There's a miniature waterfall running down the back of it, but it's the only place to belay.

I'm in a very awkward position on a single sloping foothold. I gently tap a knifeblade peg into a thin crack with my peg hammer in my left hand while holding onto the ice pick with my right. I have to be very careful, because one inaccurate hit will send it flying, lost for ever down the ravine – and we can't afford to lose a single one of our precious seven pegs, particularly our two knifeblades. As the metal starts to bite, I tap the peg a little harder, then harder still: *Ping – Ping – PING!*

You can always tell how good a peg is by the sound it makes when you hammer it in: it should be a series of rising notes. It's important not to over hit it. Now, after just three blows, it hits a restriction and won't go in any further. So I leave it at that, even though there's a lot still protruding from the rock. Then I put a short tape sling round it with a clove hitch, pressing the knot tight against the rock so that there's the minimum amount of leverage, and clip the rope into it. Fortunately, there's a shallow slot in the rock a bit higher that I can get a nut jammed into, and then there's the long-winded procedure of tying in the ropes so that the tension is just right. My calf muscle is screaming from standing with all my weight on my right foot, but at last, after about ten minutes, I've constructed a scarcely adequate belay, and can turn round to face outwards and take some of my weight on the belay ropes, with an enormous drop beneath me. I lean back in the horrible sloping wet slot, using the slab behind me as a kind of seat, so my backside soon gets very wet from the icy water. The stream is obviously the main outlet of meltwater from the huge snowfield that lies out of

Gordon constructing the belay in the watery slot on the far side of "the ravine"

sight somewhere directly above me. It really is a very nasty place. The sooner we get out of here the better.

John has been extremely patient, and now I discover what he's been up to while I've been rigging the belay. Taking photographs! He's not even holding the ropes – they're just draped around his waist while he concentrates on his photography. The camera is Dad's old Leica, which he's given to John because he is the more scientifically-minded of the two of us, and Dad sees photography as more of a science than an art.

Before John can start climbing we have to go through a time-honoured ritual of special calls.

"Taking in!" I say as I begin to take in the slack. John puts the camera away, and helps feed the rope out until it eventually comes tight on his waist.

"That's me!"

I put a twist of rope round my wrist going to the pile of spare rope at my feet, have one final check – tugging at my belay slings to see that everything's tight – then say: "Climb when you're ready!"

John dismantles his belay, putting the sling over his shoulder.

"Climbing!"

"OK."

Always those ten words, always just the same. The rule is that the second man never starts climbing until he hears that last "OK", which is the final reassurance that the leader is tending the ropes properly and is ready to hold him in the event of a fall. The calls are most reassuring in that they transform any pitch, however daunting, into a standardised routine. We might just as well now be on a rock climb in North Wales. Yet the old familiar script seems totally incongruous in this savage setting. My language, even my voice, sounds very strange in these alien surroundings. It's a bit like being in a school play and declaiming the well-rehearsed words for the first time in front of a large audience of parents and strangers. It probably wouldn't sound any dafter now to sing these climbing calls, rather than shout them. After all, as one old wit famously said of opera, what is too stupid to be said can always be sung.

"Don't tug me!" John cries, as he edges his way very slowly and carefully along the traverse line on the opposite side of the zawn. "Just leave the yellow rope absolutely slack!" This kind of pitch is equally as serious for the second as the leader because the rope cannot provide any security from above. Indeed, it often feels scarier seconding a traverse rather than a vertical pitch, particularly if the leader is out of sight and forgets to take in the rope gently enough.

When John eventually reaches me, he sees that I'm getting very wet in my watery slot, so wastes little time in going into the lead on the rather smooth-looking slab that lies ahead. He simply tiptoes up it in his big new Super Gratton boots. It looks delicate, but we've had some good practice recently on the Idwal Slabs, and on a classic old Very Severe called "Holly Tree Wall", which we managed to do in our old bendy hill-walking boots. Well, we've both got much better boots now.

When John's reached a safe ledge and tied himself on, and we've gone through all the climbing calls again, I'm secretly rather shocked to discover just how "thin" and precarious the climbing is. ("Thin" is a climbing term for something that has virtually no positive holds and relies almost entirely on friction and balance.) The rock is also unnervingly dirty and mossy, with a rather gritty texture – very dark but flecked with silver mica crystals. Biotite, I think it's called. The edges of the hard rubber soles of my brand new boots bite well into the crystals as I place them very precisely on small rugosities, but all I can see below my toe caps is the scree nearly two thousand feet below, framed by the ravine walls. Well, I've no idea how far it is really, but it's a long, long way. This is a near vertical "walk" on quartz crystals in which the battle over gravity is won more by faith and friction than by physics and actual holds. I try to make it look as easy as I can, hiding from John just how hard I'm really finding it. I'm starting to fear that the route may not be quite as easy as we've been led to believe, both by hearsay and the guidebook – which doesn't even mention this part of the climb. In fact, I'm starting to develop a certain distrust for the guidebook.

10.30 am

Well, now we're in a shallow, rubble-filled gully, with our first obstacle safely behind us; but it's taken us over an hour and a half, and we haven't even started the real climbing yet. But at least we've passed our "entrance exam", and are on our way at last – and it feels very much *one way*, because those ravine pitches would be very tricky to reverse.

Although the gully we've entered is little more than a rubbly walk, the bottom edge of the snowfield is hanging directly over us in a most threatening manner – a twenty-foot-high overhanging wall of snow-ice, dripping with melt water and having all the appearance of being about to break off any minute. As soon as we can, we scurry leftwards, up onto a broad ridge of good rock.

We are now in a truly stupendous position. The monstrous Troll Wall, blotting out the sky, looks vaster than ever, and its myriad of overhangs has grown accordingly. And – very close at hand, extraordinarily amplified by the huge semi-circular reflector bowl of the Wall – we can hear voices and the distinct metallic tinkling of karabiners. It's a most peculiar phenomenon. It takes us a second or two to realize that the sounds are coming from over half a mile away, somewhere high on the Troll Pillar, bounding the Troll Wall on the left. It's obviously Bill and Tony, the climbers we met last night.

We scan the face for a while. Eventually John spots them. They're nowhere near where the sound is coming from, but quite a lot higher: two tiny little red specks on the left side of the enormous final groove of one of the biggest rock buttresses in Europe. They're a whole rope length apart, but it looks about a centimetre. They've made amazingly good progress, but I suppose they've been climbing non-stop since about four in the morning, about the time we left our tent.

Hearing their voices is strangely unnerving. The proximity of other English climbers, sounding as if they're only about a hundred feet away, should make our undertaking feel a lot more convivial, but it doesn't. Rather the reverse, as there is such an enormous gulf between us. We are two entirely separate climbing parties, in our own entirely separate worlds, completely cut off from each other.

Everything about the Trolltindane is so strange. Even the light is strange, bathing everything now in a sickly gloom, full of shadowy secrets, weird acoustics and fragmented voices, as if the Trolls themselves are chuckling at us, even though the petrified monsters fringing the skyline are utterly lifeless, and have been frozen like that for aeons, like a terracotta army.

We stop for only a minute or two, because we still have a long way to go – judging by Bill and Tony, dispiritingly high above us on their Pillar. But where exactly does *our* route go? It's very far from obvious. Directly above us is the massive near-vertical Pillar of Brudgommen, towering mind-numbingly above our heads for nearly three thousand feet.

I think I can see the minute speck of some enormous bird that looks remarkably like a condor, wheeling around that remote, inaccessible rock turret. I point it out to John, but as soon as I mention it, it disappears. Maybe I imagined it.

I get the guidebook out of the lid of my sack, and read aloud:

"'Continue up the small left gully or its left wall (dependent on conditions) for several hundred feet, passing difficulties on the left till a steep crag is reached. Pass below this moving right into the main gully'…"

"I don't get this thing about the left wall and passing difficulties on the left," says John. "There's not much on the left – apart from the Troll Wall!"

"So we go up the left gully," I say.

We're glad the guidebook doesn't tell us to get into the main gully yet, because it appears to start as a repulsively steep black, slimy corner. Just to reach it we would have to cross the giant snowfield on our right, which must be four hundred feet wide and about five hundred feet high – the guidebook's "snow patch"! And, although it's quite easy-angled, it looks rather rotten, and has a huge bergschrund (or, crack between it and the rock) at its top edge. That the bergschrund is so obvious from here means that it must be at least twenty feet wide when you get there. Which implies that the whole melting snowfield is edging slowly downwards and may slide off the mountain at any moment …

So we head up the rib on the left side of the snowfield, aiming for the "small left gully". To start with it's very straightforward, climbing on easy-angled rock with a huge abyss on the left and the ever-present screen of the Troll Wall, incomprehensibly vast, moving up with us out of the corners of our eyes as we climb. Trying to freak us out. The only thing to do is just ignore it, unnerving as it is, on the edge of our vision.

We make rapid progress, and I cheer myself up by thinking that at this rate we'll be at the top in a few more hours.

12.10 pm

We've reached much steeper ground, still on surprisingly good rock, but above things don't look nearly so encouraging. John has gained a ledge below a much steeper buttress that in effect forms the base of the Pillar of Brudgommen.

"I'm there … there … there!" he calls. An extraordinary echo bounces back from the huge vertical south wall of Store Trolltind high on our right – the Big Troll, reminding us of his continual presence, watching over our every move.

"Taking in … in … in …!"

"Climbing … ing … ing … " I answer. And so does Mr Troll. Herr Troll.

Heil Trolltind!

"OK … ok … ok! … " John's voice echoes back.

Sieg Heil! I give a little Nazi salute.

"Do you think this is the 'steep crag' yet?" John asks when I reach him.

"I can see lots of steep crags! What a ridiculous comment! It would make a fun competition, wouldn't it? Count the number of 'steep crags' on the Fiva Route!"

Still, this seems as good a place as any to move rightwards into "the small left gully", we decide, and I lead off.

After a while I look down and find that John has his camera out again, and is belaying me with one hand, with the whole of Romsdal spread out behind him. He has pulled out a lot of slack, not expecting me to fall off, it seems. His whole manner exudes confidence and an extraordinary indifference to his awesome surroundings. There are times when he can be quite a good actor.

I look up to my right, and to my astonishment spot a little triangular spike of a cairn on the skyline that forms the right side of the gully. It's the very last thing I was expecting to see. I tell John.

"Where … where … where …?"

"You can't see it until you get up here … uphere … uphere … "

"Well, that's obviously where we traverse right into the main gully … ully … ully. It's obviously a route marker … arker … arker…!"

12.30 pm

The cairn is unquestionably a bit of a riddle. Why is it so big and so well constructed? It's about four feet high and three feet in diameter, suggesting that a lot of people have passed this way. Or perhaps it was built by just one team of cairn-constructing fanatics? There are a couple of very old rusty tin cans lying next to it, implying that some people at least have bivvied here. Maybe they built the cairn more or less for fun, simply as a memento of having stayed here?

Again, the cans are strangely disturbing rather than encouraging. They're just so very old, suggesting no one's actually been here for years. Perhaps they're even remnants of Heen's first ascent, dating all the way back to 1931? It's a bit like meeting a ghost, or some old bones. One certainly half expects to find a skeleton lying around here somewhere.

"I think the cairn's a route marker," John decides. "And it's been deliberately put here so that it can be seen from the left-hand gully. I think this must be Tony Howard's 'steep crag', and we go right into the main gully here."

"I don't know. I don't think we've climbed nearly high enough yet."

"The cairn *has* to be some kind of marker," John insists – "telling us to traverse right."

So we go all the way along the broad grassy terrace to its right-hand end and peer into the main gully. It looks horrendous – a dark, narrow cleft filled with very steep rotten snow.

John takes one look at it and says, "No way! Only a loony would go in there!"

We know from the guidebook that a Norwegian and two Swedes were killed here three years ago attempting the route in winter. It's an obvious death trap, and it's clearly now in a lethal condition.

"It's a pity," I say, "because the actual snow looks like it would be about Scottish Grade I if it was in good nick."

"Well, it's out of the question now," John insists. "It looks like it's in avalanche condition … I'm not going up there! Only complete nutters would ever go up a thing like that."

"It certainly does look very rotten …"

"No, we must avoid that like the plague." It's a surprisingly posh expression for John to use in such coarse surroundings, and he says it in a very posh voice, as he always does when he's being very serious. He's copying Dad, really. "It doesn't tie up with the guidebook description anyway," he adds. "We'd have to abseil in, to get into it. The cairn must mean the route goes somewhere up the buttress behind it."

So we go back to the cairn and try to climb the steep wall behind it. It's my turn to lead again. I have quite a lot of trouble getting started, but eventually manage to teeter up a steep slabby groove for about fifteen feet on friction. The rock is very smooth, very "thin" again. It's much harder than anything you would expect on a Grade IV climb, with no signs of anyone ever having been this way before. It's obviously climbable, but potentially very dangerous because it's very blind, with no friendly cracks for protection, no obvious holds or ledges, and nothing obvious to aim for. What if it gets harder higher up?

I come down and John has a go. Eventually he comes down too. "If it was in the Alps," he says, "I'm sure there would be a peg or something, even if simply as a marker."

There is another possible line, another shallow groove in the rock about twenty feet to the right of the cairn, but on closer inspection we find it to be even less amenable than the first. Again, it's going to be very "run out", with next to no available protection, no spikes for slings or any cracks for nuts. Which means it's virtually as dangerous as climbing it without a rope. Again John goes up just a few feet, and then stops.

"Do you want a go?"

"No. You'd better come down." If John can't do it, I'm sure I won't be able to.

Then we go back and try immediately behind the cairn again, but again without success.

"How about just to the left?"

"No, that looks even worse."

There's a fear in our voices now that neither of us can completely conceal, and it's contagious. We're infecting each other with our doubts. Something extraordinary has happened in the last few minutes. All our confidence seems to have evaporated into thin air. Just six weeks ago we were climbing "Very Severe" routes in our bendy hill-walking boots – in the cold, in the snow, for Christ's sake! – and now what? We suddenly seem incapable of doing anything. We've lost all momentum, and can scarcely get our feet off this big terrace … on a route that was first done in 1931! *What is going on?* Where is this negative magnetic force coming from that's driving us back? This is a stronger force than gravity, because it comes from within, and compounds gravity, working in league with it. We are now as much up against our own fears and doubts as the mountain itself.

It's as if the route is teasing us. Nothing is obvious any more. An air of mystery hangs over the whole enterprise. The cairn shows that people have certainly been here, yet the rock above us has an extraordinarily unclimbed look and feel about it. It's hard to explain. The whole vibe that the mountain is giving out is that the route does *not* go up behind the cairn. There might just as well be a big sign up here saying "No Entry" or "Access Forbidden to Unauthorised Novices", or …

"Abandon All Hope All Ye Who Enter Here."

Stop this, Gordon!

"It can't go here," I say.

"Well, it must do," counters John, reasonably. "Where else?"

"Well, there *is* the left-hand gully. The guidebook doesn't say anything about climbing any ridge or buttress. It's all about the left-hand gully to start with. We *could* try carrying on up that for a bit. It didn't look at all bad to me."

John agrees. "The guidebook says 'continue up the left gully for several hundred feet' and we probably haven't gone high enough yet. I think the cairn could be a complete red herring!"

So the left-hand gully it is.

2.30 pm

Like a couple of inquisitive beetles that have wandered
inadvertently into a hidden crack and have nowhere to go but up,
we are now deeply immersed in one of the mountain's most secret
crevices, clambering over, around, and sometimes under, huge
chockstones – enormous boulders jammed in a near-vertical slimy
cleft (in climbing terms, a "chimney"), reeking with damp moss.
Crawling ever upwards into the very bowels of the dinosaur.

I'm leading again and, much to my relief, the climbing, though
steep and strenuous, is quite easy and my spirits have soared. At
last we're making good progress. Although there's no evidence
that anyone's ever been this way before, it involves nothing more
than standard "chimneying" techniques, a kind of vertical caving.
Much of the time I'm "bridging", climbing with one foot on one
wall and one on the other, using whatever footholds I can find
on the greasy vertical rock, while my hands grapple with huge
wet chockstones wedged across the cleft. Sometimes these force
me out a long way towards the front of the cleft – so that it's
surprisingly exposed, with smooth walls dropping into an abyss
– presenting me with a series of strenuous overhangs that have to
be surmounted, usually with good handholds. But sometimes the
holds disappear completely, which means I have to get myself into
a classic "chimneying" position, with my body jammed across the
void as if I'm sitting on an invisible chaise longue, with my back
on one wall and my feet on the other. And it's made all the more
precarious and awkward by the fact that I've got my sack on my
back with my ice axe strapped to it. To move up, I have to bring one
foot back onto the rock behind me – say, my right foot – and push
myself up and away from the wall with my hands, while levering
up on the right foot behind me until my left foot is outstretched
across the ravine to the limit of its adhesion. Then I stick my right
foot back across the ravine, but much higher now – so high that
my heavy metal peg hammer threatens to fall out of the slot in my
breeches – and bring my left foot up beside it. And then I rest with
my bum against the wet wall, my body jammed across the cleft, and

my ice axe grating against the rock.

It's a most peculiar, reptilian form of upward progress, and hot and steamy work with it as I'm still wearing my anorak, which is becoming ever damper from the wet rock. In climbing parlance it's what we call "graunchy" or "thrutchy". The two terms are subtly different, "thrutchy" being even more awkward and strenuous than "graunchy". This is merely invigoratingly graunchy. And, dare I say it? Even though it's bloody strenuous, the truth is that it's quite fun really, a bit like clambering up the inside of a huge children's climbing frame.

In a strange kind of way it's also quite reminiscent of our first innocent tree-climbing days, which represented our first real grapplings with nature, when we first had a sense of coming to grips with the very stuff of life … We started to take tree climbing much more seriously three years ago, once we started rock climbing; and the trees of Knebworth Park offered the only real climbing possibilities for miles around. We found the very hard smooth bark of hornbeams to be full of very rock-like finger pockets, cracks and knobs, providing a whole range of hard technical climbing problems, often involving very strenuous rounded laybacks up overhanging ribs … They were good days, good evenings … in the evening sun in Knebworth Park …

At last, when I've climbed nearly the full one-hundred-and-fifty-foot rope length up this huge dark, lavatorial slot, I arrive at a flat platform on top of a massive chockstone and tie myself on. When it comes to John's turn to second it, I can tell that he's finding it very easy because I have to take in the rope almost as fast as I can. Which is just as well, because this is not the sort of place we want to stay in for a moment longer than we have to. It feels very claustrophobic sitting in this dark slit in the mountainside, completely cut off from the rest of the world. All I can see, framed between the vertical walls of this slimy chimney, is the huge four-thousand-foot sombre, vegetated rock-face of the Romsdalshorn directly opposite me on the other side of the valley.

John's head pops over the edge of the great chockstone boulder with a big grin. He pulls a face. "Very severe!" he says, imitating Aunt Hazel when she arrived back with Dad after their ascent of the Matterhorn. She was absolutely grey with fatigue, and all she could do was mutter "Very severe! Very severe!" over and over again. What he means now is dead easy, or a piece of piss. ("Very Severe" is, of course, a British rock climbing grade that's many times harder than anything to be found on the Hörnli Ridge of the Matterhorn, and it has now become something of a private joke for John and me to say "Very Severe" in Aunt Hazel's voice whenever we climb a particularly easy pitch.)

John storms into the lead again in high spirits, his legs bridged across the rock walls directly above my head.

3.30 pm

On and on it goes. I've been climbing up the dark confines of this chimney system for nearly three hundred feet, trapped in my own vertical sweaty world as I clamber over and around huge gravelly chockstones, cut off completely from any traces of civilization. But at last the angle begins to ease.

John is out of sight above me, belaying. It's all very silent. Come to think of it, John's been very silent ever since he's reached the top of this pitch, and the only evidence I have that I am not alone in the world is that the rope is being taken in very attentively, accurately reflecting my every jerky upward move.

All at once I emerge onto a snow patch where the angle sets back and the gully widens out into a gigantic open-topped funnel – and I find myself looking at a stupendous "Lost World" worthy of Conan Doyle. All that's lacking are pterodactyls circling overhead.

Ye gods!

My jaw drops as I gaze upwards at a great steep-walled amphitheatre, like a beetle looking up from the base of an earthenware pot that's been sliced in half and topped by the stupendous two-thousand-foot Pillar of Brudgommen towering into the sky above me. The great back wall of this Norwegian Lost

World of Roraima is daubed with several giant black, vertical water streaks that enforce the impression of impregnability. But, in place of any waterfall, indeed just where one might expect there to be a waterfall, is a single sharp-edged crack, probably a hundred and fifty feet high and absolutely vertical. Above it, to the left, forming the substructure, as it were, of the Pillar of Brudgommen, like the *corbels* supporting a gigantic Gothic turret – yes, I have just done an A-Level in Architecture – lurching crazily outwards against the sky, is a series of savage overhangs, much like an upside-down staircase.

The crack appears to be very narrow, perhaps not much more than a foot wide, so it's not immediately obvious that one can even get inside it – and even if one could crawl in there, like an ungainly insect trying to obtain lodgement between the jaws of an ancient vice, it looks very black and slimy, reminding me of an old broken drainpipe – an impression that's made all the stronger by the way it takes a sharp dog-leg to the right about half-way up, so that it looks as if the whole wall has been cleaved in two by a single stroke of lightning.

Our route can't go up there! That looks about Hard VS or even Extreme. In fact, I very much doubt if anyone's ever been up that savage slit. It looks absolutely ferocious.

John tugs impatiently at the rope, his back turned firmly on the horror behind him. He's looking down at me as if he's not even aware of it, his face grimly expressionless, giving out no message, no emotion whatever. As inscrutable as the rock itself.

"God almighty!" I exclaim. "That doesn't look very good!"

"I wondered what you'd say! It looks bloody awful, doesn't it?" He keeps his attention on me, as if refusing to look round at it.

"Where's our gully gone?" I gasp.

"I don't know…. Maybe it's not so bad", he suggests, "once you get up to it."

"But it can't go up there!… That looks about Hard VS!…"

"It must do…! Or, there's some way off to the right that we can't see yet."

"What does that bloody guidebook say again?" John asks when I join him. He's sounding quite cross now.

I get it out of the lid of my sack again – even though I know it virtually by heart now – and read:

"*'Continue up the small left gully or its left wall (dependent on conditions) for several hundred feet, passing difficulties on the left'* – "

"Yes, yes, yes," John snaps – "we've done that bit! 'Till a steep crag is reached'."

I continue: "*'Pass below this moving right into the main gully and escaping by a hole and chimney to Ugla Skar'.*" The writing is so esoteric that it's quite difficult to read.

"Well we can't *'move right into the gully'*," John says, really sarcastic now – "there's a whole bloody buttress in the way! And 'pass below a steep crag!' – that has to be one of the silliest expressions I've ever seen in a guidebook. I mean, just how many 'steep crags' have we passed already!"

"I wouldn't even call it a crag – it's more like a huge amphitheatre. It's all 'steep crag', for Christ's sake!"

"It's strange that it doesn't even mention the crack – which is by far the most obvious feature. What a peculiar guidebook!" John scowls.

"Well, if that's the 'steep crag', there has to be some hidden traverse off to the right somewhere."

So we decide to go up and have a look. Neither of us so much as suggests climbing the crack. Something as absurdly fierce as that can't possibly be on the correct route.

I go back into the lead up easy-angled slabby rock in the gully bed, and then head up to the right to a dark recess below the most broken part of the buttress, with that hideous vertical slot hanging above me on the left, bristling with overhangs and menace. John joins me and, taking all the ironmongery from me, carries on up steeper rock, searching for some kind of weakness that will let us escape to the right-hand edge of the fortress that encloses us. He starts moving very slowly to the right above some blocky overhangs far above me, nearly outlined against the sky, until he's perched on

The left-hand gully with the main gully on the right. C = the cairned terrace, scarcely visible from this distance. J = John's high point right of the "lightning crack."

a strange-looking pulpit-type feature with near-vertical rock above him. I note that he's on a very "steep crag" indeed. It all looks very scary, and quite absurd for a "Grade Four" route.

An inner voice is already screaming at me that we mustn't go up there, because we're bound to get into all kinds of trouble if we do. Yet it's so important in climbing never to be daunted by appearances. You always have to remain as cool and as objective

about the difficulties as you possibly can. Intuitions so often prove
to be false.

Patience, Gordon! … But I feel a tightening knot of fear in my
stomach. Something in my guts is telling me that there's something
very wrong about this. Despite all my efforts to keep emotionally
cool and detached, huge doubts are setting in.

After a while I venture: "What's it like?" – my nervous voice
sounding ever so small – and all-too-human.

"I'm not sure … ure … I can't see yet … yet … It doesn't look very far
… ar …" John's voice wafts down from the hideous heights above,
trailing off into the vastness of the amphitheatre.

"It can't go up there, John! It looks about Hard VS."

"It doesn't look so bad close up … up …" comes the strangely echoing
reply. "It might go with some aid … aid …"

"But it's meant to be Severe, for God's sake! It can't go up there.
It looks far too hard!" I'm shouting at the rock in front of my
face to avoid getting a crick in my neck looking up at John on his
pedestal in the sky. You can almost smell my fear now, and it seems
my doubts are being transmitted like a silent poison up the rope
because, despite John's vocal optimism, the rope remains resolutely
stationary.

I look at my watch.

Christ Almighty! The hands have flipped round to four-thirty – as
if my watch has got a mind of its own now and is playing tricks
with me in league with the mountain. Two and a half hours have
gone since we started up this left-hand gully. We've already been
on the go for over eleven hours, and we're obviously still nowhere
near the top…. Gosh that watch looks silly now: so absurdly out of
place, so absurdly twee and refined in this crude, gargantuan setting
– sitting on my wrist as if I'm still in our "drawing-room" back
home in Knebworth in Hertfordshire. Still trying to pretend that it
has some kind of relevance in this time-contemptuous domain of
the Trolls – when in fact it's clearly full of treachery, and working
now in partnership with them.

Suddenly I'm feeling very panicky. I'm really getting to hate this spot. I doubt if you dug down ten thousand feet below the chalk of Hertfordshire you'd come across anything quite as primitive as this, it's just so intimidating. And I start to scream up at John on his horrible perch, telling him to come down, this is ridiculous! "The route can't possibly go up there. We must be off route. We're just wasting time! It's nearly quarter to five, and at this rate we're going to have our time cut out to get to the top and get to Stegfoss tonight … night … "

At this moment, just when it seems my doubts cannot become more acute, I feel drizzle on my face again, as if nature is contriving to wash away the very last vestiges of my confidence. It's as if it's suddenly saying to us: "Give up! … *Go down!"*

"There's a flakey wall here … here … " comes the small, distant voice. "… Some small cracks that might take pegs … pegs … " I can't catch it all.

"But that's ridiculous on something that's meant to be a Grade Four! We can't be on the right route … oute …!"

John ignores me. He calls down: "Have you got the other knifeblade … lade …? There's some flakes that look as if they could take knifeblades … lades … " He seems rather insistent.

"Yes – but I'm using it for the belay!"

I think I can just hear John say to himself quietly, "Damn!"

I'm now looking across the steep slabs to my right. Maybe there's a way across there?

More time passes, and then I'm shouting up at him again, "Please John, let's try to find the proper route! … oute!… " I'm almost begging him to come down.

I think I hear a distant "OK"; and at last, very slowly and rather reluctantly, he starts to climb down. I take in the rope, fielding him to safety.

"It's really annoying that," he says, once he joins me, looking remarkably unfazed. "With the right pegs you could probably get up quite easily. It only looked about twenty feet or thirty feet to get to easier ground."

"But we haven't got enough pegs," I remind him.

"Well, what do you suggest?" He looks drained now.

"I've been looking over to the right – at that line of flakes. What do you think?"

John appears very dubious. "… Umm … I'm not sure …"

It's still spotting lightly with rain.

"But the crest over there looks so friendly," I say. "If only we could get out there, I'm sure all will be revealed … Otherwise we're going to have to go the whole way back to the cairn, and we don't want to do that …"

"Well, do you want to have a look?" John offers. "Why don't you give it a whirl? I'll belay you."

"OK."

It's very much my turn again now. John has obviously expended a lot of adrenaline, and now it's over to me to try and pull something out of the bag.

We swap belays in the gloomy recess and I take all the slings and pegs and start to edge my way very gingerly out onto a huge steep, slabby apron of friable rock on the side of the gully, carefully testing every hold … making my way along a line of little finger slats and brittle ledges. It's very unfriendly, but the promise of the spiky, solid-looking skyline lures me on. We *must* try and get up there.

The line of flakes runs out, but there's another just a few feet higher. A couple of precarious moves gets me established in balance on it, then I carry on more or less as before.

Oops! A whole flake, about an inch thick, hinges out like a heavy stone tile. I tap it back, then feel along the edge with my fingers to solid rock beyond it, and soon reach a line of better holds. Which I follow all the way, slightly upwards, in an ever more airy position – with no protection at all, and the depths of Romsdal clutching at my back. The rock is all very friable, and has obviously never been touched by the hand of man … or woman! The truth is, I'm feeling very much like an old woman now – a *Trollkjerringa* – because, although I'm making steady progress, I haven't felt this uncertain on a rock climb for a very long time. It's hard to believe that only six weeks ago I was climbing confidently at Very Severe standard on Great Slab on Cloggy, in bad conditions in the drizzle. The climbing here is very similar, but I'm just feeling so different, so very feeble. All gripped up.

John's voice booms out, bouncing around the walls: "Can you belay there? ... air ... You haven't got much rope left ... left ... "

"How much?"

"About twenty feet ... feet ... "

But there is no belay at all, not even a hairline crack; so I have to carry on. Then the line of flakes disappears. I'm on a good ledge, but there's a smooth shield of rock in front of me, with the skyline tantalisingly close beyond it, not much more than forty feet away. Directly above me there are hints of holds, but it's much steeper, sterner stuff. It looks about VS, but it's really not very far at all. John should be able to get up that – if only I can find something suitable to belay on. If I can find just *one* spike, or *one* crack, our troubles could soon be over. But there is absolutely nothing. It really is the most peculiarly alien place. I have no choice now but to start edging back towards John, who's sitting patiently in his gloomy alcove about a hundred and thirty feet away. I search all the way for something to anchor myself to, fiddling with nuts in blind furrows, draping slings over shallow, flat-topped flakes, but nothing works. Never in all my three years of climbing have I come across such an uncooperative sheet of rock.

I get back to the lower line of flakes and ledges. Surely *here* there must be something, some kind of nut placement or spike? I get out a knifeblade peg and start to bang it down a hairline crack behind a flake in front of me. It gives a dull *pung!* sound, and the whole thing snaps and hinges away from the mountain like a soft biscuit, leaving a smooth patch of sandy-looking orange rock behind. It's all so brittle. This isn't nice gneiss, this is horrible old shitty schist.

Just when I'm nearly back in the gully, only about twenty feet from John – like a very sick joke because I am now far too far from the ridge for it to be of the slightest use – I find a perfect large nut placement, a deep V-shaped slot, ideal for my aluminium MOAC wedge.

That things have started to go very wrong with our climb is to put it mildly. The horrible truth is a hundred per cent plain: we should never have come up this left-hand gully. We've been lured into a cul de sac, which is obviously nowhere near the proper route. It's as if the mountain has laid a trap for us, playing games with our psyche and, like two little beetles lured into a bottle, we've fallen right into it. This whole three-and-a-half-hour excursion has been a complete waste of time, an entirely futile, energy-sapping exercise.

The awful realization is also creeping up on me that we're running out of ideas. Surely the mountain hasn't defeated us already? It's unthinkable for us to give up.

"We've made a big mistake coming up here," John says, voicing my thoughts. "I think we should've gone right at the cairn. As I said before, I reckon it's an obvious traverse marker. I think I've been proved right now."

"Yup, I've got to agree. I've got a hunch that the main gully may be perfectly straightforward, and we've been too easily put off by appearances. And, even if it means getting into the main gully too early, it'll soon join up with the proper route, because we know that's where it goes higher up."

"OK," John says, "let's do it, and stop farting about!"

At last "the riddle of the cairn" has been solved. The beauty of our solution is that we will now definitely get onto the proper route whatever happens. We were just being spazzy about getting into the main gully earlier simply because it's in a bad condition. It should be fine if we take care. "I'm sure I'll be able to do it," I say with all the confidence of someone who's recently had the benefit of a week's expert training on a snow and ice climbing course in Glencoe. My instructors, after all, were none other than the legendary Allen Fyffe and Ian Clough.

"I'll do all the leading with my ice axe," I continue, "and you can use your peg hammer" – the point being that, although John hasn't got an ice axe, his peg hammer is unusual in having a short ice-pick on the side opposite the hammer. "It should be fine for seconding."

"Ok, I suppose so," John says after a moment's thought. "Yes."

At last rationality has kicked in – after hours of doubt and indecision. I feel an overwhelming sense of relief, amounting almost to euphoria, that we are going to get up the climb now at all costs, with a minimum of further mucking about. With my renewed hope has come a new sense of commitment. The time for dithering is over.

We retrace our reptilian contortions down the gloomy chimney with a new-found energy, like predators with the whiff of fresh prey. Even though we've wasted a lot of time, and are having to descend a long way, we've become totally focused again. I'm even feeling vaguely heroic, clambering back down over all the chockstones as nimbly and gymnastically as possible, throwing myself into all the chimneying moves that are required with a kind of exaggerated gusto that causes the pick of my ice axe to spark against the rock. This has all the feeling about it of a classic moment, a classic turning point. If I were to be very literary about it, I'd describe it as "one glorious hour of crowded life" – as one of the ancients put it. Just who was it who said that? I can't remember, it really doesn't matter now.

I'm humming, even singing, as we descend into the gloom. I often do this on a climb when I'm keyed up. It calms the nerves, and helps me concentrate, like putting a crazy smile on my face – that's another trick that really works for me – and I've got a really crazy smile on my face right now! …

7.30 pm

So it is that around seven-thirty in the evening – after nearly fifteen hours on the mountain – we're back at the by now over-familiar, enigmatic cairn. The sky to the north-east, to left of the Vengetind, is looking dark and threatening, but the rain has stopped and I'm in high spirits.

John is less sanguine. He's muttering, "That round trip's got to be the most *fruitless* bit of climbing I've ever done." He's already said this several times in the last few minutes, as if I haven't heard him. He's fond of repeating favourite words, and his theme of the moment is "fruitless".

We sit by the cairn (and those two old rusty tin cans), and have a bite to eat. We've only got three-quarters of a bar of chocolate and a couple of sandwiches left. We're now not so much fruitless as almost foodless.

"You know, we haven't brought nearly enough food," John says, staring into the food bag, echoing my thoughts, stating the obvious.

"That bloke telling us all we need is a couple of Mars Bars!" I say. "He must've been bloody joking!"

"Well, we're going to have to ration it, aren't we? Let's just have a bit of chocolate now. We need to keep up the blood sugar because it could be quite cold in the gully."

I agree. "We can have some more once we've got onto the proper route, because it should be plain sailing then."

8.00 pm

We've climbed nearly a full rope length down a steep ramp of broken rock below the terrace to a small ledge about seventy feet above the floor of the main gully, where we can look into it fully for the first time. This huge cleft in the side of Store Trolltind really deserves some name like the "Giant Troll's Cleft" or "Giant's Gateway", or something, it's just so stupendous in every way. And ominously quiet – as if it's wrapped in sleep – as if the Trolls have hung up some message for the evening saying "Do Not Disturb". The snow itself doesn't look quite so steep now from this vantage point, and appears to have a solid, icy surface – but it's hard to tell, really, because it's obviously very rotten. And it still *looks* very intimidating. The gully is, in effect, a smooth-walled gorge, not much more than fifteen feet wide down at the back of the cleft, with gigantic black walls soaring up into the gloom, the one on the far side of us extending dizzily upwards in a near-vertical rock face of withering proportions, all the way to the blunt arrow-tip of

Store Trolltind itself, thrust defiantly against the cloudy sky over two thousand feet above our heads. It's as if the whole gully has been formed by a single slash of a mile-long scimitar.

I still can't really tell how steep the snow is. It's probably only about forty-five to fifty degrees – which is much more acute than it sounds to anyone who's never been on a steep snow slope – but it's not set at a constant angle: it comes cascading towards us in a series of enormous bulges, like frozen waves that may come to life again and crash down on us any minute. But, although the snow looks repulsively rotten, I say:

"You know, I don't think it looks too bad at all! I don't think there's any real problem." As the newly styled "snow and ice expert", I try to sound as unconcerned and convincing as I possibly can.

"Are you sure?"

"Yeah … I think it's probably going to be fine. The snow looks a bit soft, but it should just be like any old standard Grade I Scottish gully."

John raises his eyebrows, as if to say, *Really?*

"I tell you what," I add: "if you just lower me down the last bit I can see what the snow's really like – and if it's really too dangerous I can always climb back up on a tied-off rope. You know, using loops – with you belaying me on the other."

"And then what?" Still sounding less than convinced.

"No, John, honestly, I think it's going to be fine. I'm sure we can do this!"

A slight sigh. "OK – if you say so!"

It's reassuring to hear John deferring to my more experienced judgement for once, based on my superior snow-climbing expertise. It's quite rare for me to be better at something than he is. It's usually the other way round.

The plan, now, is: if it looks OK, I'll untie and John'll abseil down to join me. Once we've retrieved the double ropes there will then be no escape, and we'll be completely committed to climbing the gully.

I don my thick Dachstein woollen mitts, and get the ice axe off the back of my sack and tuck it into my shoulder strap, all ready for action. I clip the end of its lanyard into my chest sling so there's no risk of dropping it.

John nods when I'm ready, "OK, good luck!" and I start climbing down a very steep, black, slimy slab of very hard old metamorphic rock (– I think it's what they call "biotite gneiss", but it's not very nice at all). John's wearing his Millar mitts now, and keeps me on a very tight rope. After about twenty feet, the holds disappear completely, and I have to lean backwards, putting my full weight on the rope, while John holds me, to stop my feet shooting off the slimy wall.

"You'd better just lower me now."

I lean back further, as John gently pays out the damp rope through his mitts until my body is in an abseil position – almost at right angles to the rock, to stop my feet from slipping on the black slime – and then slowly "walk" backwards down the wall as he lowers me. Down rock that has been polished very smooth, presumably by hundreds of thousands of years of abrasion by the ice. I can't see a single crack that would take even the thinnest peg.

I warn John: "We're definitely not going to be able to climb back out of here. There are absolutely no peg placements that I can see."

As I near the snow at the base of the ravine, I have a very strong sense of entering forbidden territory, as if I'm an SAS commando raiding an impregnable fortress. It has a strong whiff of "Where Eagles Dare" about it, with me in a starring role that I hadn't quite bargained for. There are no sentries about, but I feel as if hundreds of alien eyes are staring down at me from a great height.

Soon I find myself just above a dark shallow slot where the snow has melted away from the foot of the wall, and I tell John to keep lowering me gently, as I turn sideways so that my legs enter the slot and my feet come to rest on a small rock ledge in the gloom. It all feels extremely inhospitable, a feeling that is only intensified by a chill damp updraft in the back of the gully, as if I've been lowered into a freezer that's being defrosted, with everything dripping with a cold clamminess that clings to the ice, the rock, my clothing and my woollen mitts. The air temperature can only be just above freezing, since I can see my own breath and the ventile fabric of my anorak is filmed with dew.

"OK, give me a very tight rope!" I call up. "I'm going to test the snow."

I get my ice axe out and, taking all my weight on the ropes with my left hand, I lean sideways as far as I can over the snow slope on my right. Then I cut a small handhold with the adze of my axe in the snow just above my head – and I get a bit of a shock. Although the surface is coated with ice, as I expected, it's very thin, and the snow underneath is as soft as wet sugar. It has just the same rotten texture as the snow bank I traversed this morning in the first ravine, only worse. It's truly awful stuff, softened further by another long day of warmer weather. Just why was I expecting it to be any different? Why on earth should it surprise me?

But the real moment of truth is yet to come. *Will it take my weight?*

I thrust the pick of my ice axe temporarily into the snow to park it, and put my woollen-mitted hand into the little hole I've cut, digging down with my fingers so that the edge of the ice forms a sharp-edged hold like a slender rung. I pull down harder on it, testing it. It feels surprisingly firm. I put a little more weight on it. Still it holds firm. Now I reach out with my right foot and kick my toe into the icy surface of the snow beneath me. It cracks immediately into a concave recess, like a thick eggshell that's been hit by a spoon. I give a second light kick, and my foot goes through the brittle ice into the soft interior. Grasping my delicate handhold like an upended plate, I shift my weight over onto my right foot and it immediately crunches down about nine inches, breaking the ice crust below … and then stops. It's taking most of my weight, but it still feels very precarious, very fragile indeed.

With some of my weight being taken by the tight rope provided by John – like a dangling puppet that's become caught up in a piece of flimsy stage scenery – I carefully take my hand out of the icy hold and grasp the top of my ice axe like a dagger. Then I take my left hand off the ropes and put it into the vacated hand slot.

"OK, give me a little bit of slack!" I yelp.

I take my left foot swiftly off the rock and place it next to my right, kicking it into the snow alongside. I deliberately jump up and down very gently on the holds, feeling my feet settle a little further.

My body is now completely suspended by four points of contact in the crusty surface of the marshmallow snow, the rope slack. My full body weight is held by the thin skin of ice. Good. Very good. It's going to work. *If* I'm very careful!

I stand with all my weight being taken on my feet now, getting used to the feel of it, and looking down quite deliberately to stare fair and square at the snow slope beneath me disappearing, convex, out of sight into the great sucking gulf of air below. Getting used to the unexpected sense of exposure, the feeling of insecurity, and detachment from terra firma. Like a precarious marionette stuck foolishly on the side of a giant meringue.

"What's it like?" John calls down in the gloom, his voice sounding surprisingly close, not echoing at all here.

"It's OK," I paraphrase. "It's got a good icy surface that takes all my weight. It's not just soft snow … It'll definitely go."

"Oh, good."

I don't tell John that just above me the rotten snow bulges out into a near-vertical wall about fifteen feet high. But I'm confident I can do it.

I put my right hand back into the sugary handhold, tell John in an authoritative tone to "Take in", and step nimbly back onto the rock ledge. Fortunately, just in front of my face there's a very convenient large, solid rock flake with a good crack behind it; and in a moment I have my favourite MOAC securely wedged in it, and myself clipped in. Just for good measure, I put another nut in the crack to make myself doubly safe, and clip in to that too.

"OK, I'm unroping now, and you can haul up the ropes … Wait a sec!…"

It's a scary moment, this, as I undo the two figure-of-eight knots attaching my climbing ropes to my waist karabiner, call "OK", and John hauls them up, the ends disappearing out of sight, leaving me entirely alone in the world, attached to the mountain only by two small metal wedges jammed into a cold damp crack.

While John, perched somewhere high above me, is preparing the abseil rope, I am left utterly alone in a black-and-white world of rock and snow and dripping icicles that is completely devoid of life, yet filled with an oppressive silence that clings around me like the cold itself. But it's worse than that – because now I realize that this refrigerated "Hall of the Mountain King" is not completely silent. For I can hear a very faint, distant soft murmuring of running water coming up from the slot between the rock and the snow, verifying that the gully snow-ice has been melting further today, and is now satiated with menace. It's like an incessant burble of whispering voices, as if a lot of children are chattering excitedly deep under the snow, discussing my intrusion into their playground in sing-song voices. A myriad of Norwegian fairies with Welsh accents:

… silly people … think they can? … can they? Ha! … Ha ha ha! … Bold ones coming t'walk the gangplank … silly plonkers crossing th'bar …

Off-putting as it is, I try to ignore it. I take off my sack, clipping it to the belay sling, and don my red cagoule, partly for extra warmth and partly to keep out some of the all-pervasive damp. But the excited commentary from the Troll playground below carries on regardless, full of carping innuendo:

… Would you believe it? … Silly novices playing death-dice … Cheeky plonkers – ha, ha, ha! … What a giggle, silly buggers! … Flimsy psychos jangling nervy … Jelly babies wobbling skywards … ha, ha, ha! …

"Below!"

There is a scurrying, flapping sound and the two ends of the rope come tumbling down the very steep slabby wall towards me and end up in a great pile of coils at my feet. I grab the yellow and red strands and separate them.

"OK, test it!" John calls. "Pull the red!"

I pull the red rope like a bell pull. It's quite stretchy, and there's some friction, but I can feel it moving, and … sure enough, the yellow half of the rope alongside it starts going up the slippery wall in the opposite direction. Which means we can retrieve the rope without it becoming jammed. One of the more serious mishaps that can befall you on a mountain is to get an abseil rope stuck.

"OK," I call, "that's fine!"

A moment later John is abseiling down the slippery slab towards me – "God, these walls are ice-smoothed!" he says – and soon we are both perched on the little ledge next to the snow, clipped to the single belay sling.

"You realize when we pull these ropes we'll be completely committed?" John says in an almost threatening way.

"Yes."

"OK," he says, and we both haul as hard as we can on the red rope – as fast and as smoothly as possible, keeping up the momentum of the rope running through the hemp abseil sling that John has left hanging round a large spike. In a matter of seconds, the yellow rope disappears up the wall, and we keep pulling and pulling on the red rope, hand over hand – its colour changing to yellow as the half-way point is passed – until suddenly it goes slack and the whole of the rest of the rope comes snaking down the rock wall, landing on top of us in festoons.

… Ha, ha, ha! … Little mice men wrapped in tinsel! … Peeping toms in Compton helmets! … prying pranksters flushing toilets … blundering piddlers wetting trousers … notwithstanding … Proper Charlies, ha, ha, ha! … Ha, ha, ha!

Now we're totally committed.

The great Scots climber, Tom Patey, who came up this very gully nine years ago when he made an unsuccessful attempt at a first winter ascent of the Fiva Route, has written a witty article about climbing terminology, with his own rather special brand of black humour. My favourite is when he translates "Amusing" (a term much beloved of rock-climbing guidebook writers) as "Die laughing". His rendering of "committed" is rather less humourous: "Under Suspended Sentence of Death".

I wish I hadn't thought of that now.

John looks at me steadily. "You really reckon this is OK?"

"Yes, the ice is surprisingly firm. I'm sure it's going to be fine."

I hope my tone doesn't sound just a little too breezy.

At that moment there is a fierce whining, humming sound, almost like someone turning on one of those new small electric drills for a second or two – and a rock about the size of a grapefruit goes whizzing past us at terminal velocity, not much more than ten or fifteen feet out in space behind us. Not unlike a cannonball, really.

"Christ on a bicycle! – I don't like the look of *that!*" John says with emphasis.

"I think anything that comes down is going to be too far out in space to hit us," I surmise. "They won't reach us." I'm really making it up as I go along, because it's just so important not to show my fear, not to show just how vulnerable I actually feel. Though it is, of course, extremely difficult to hide *anything* from a twin brother. Who looks at me rather sternly, as if he doesn't quite follow my logic. John the Scientist. But neither of us mentions the subject again, and we start to ready ourselves for the task ahead.

John puts his blue cagoule on over his anorak, then reminds me that we've got our snow gaiters with us. "Could be a good idea here." Yes, great, I agree. The big snag with this is that you have to take your boots off in order to put your gaiters on. We sit down on the cold, wet rock ledge, and very carefully remove our boots. I place mine gently on the ledge beside me, tie the laces together, and temporarily attach them to a sling clipped into my waistband. John does the same. It's a very serious maneouvre, because a dropped boot now would be absolutely catastrophic. You could hardly imagine a more disastrous mishap to befall you on a big climb such as this.

I pull the thick grey tubular canvas gaiters up over my feet and calves, and put my boots on again. Then I take off my woollen mitts to do up my laces – which all takes time – so my fingers get very cold – while the water sprites babble their perpetual commentary:

… English pixies coming twinly … defying physics with fumbling fingers … naughty novices lacing dance shoes … tawdry dawdlers in mortal danger … plucking

fiddlers warbling wetly … gullible bummers spouting nonsense … wishful thinking …
Would you believe it? … Coming up here? … Coming up here? … Ha, ha, ha!

I hook the bottom of my gaiters to my laces with their metal clips, then tie their retaining straps under my insteps. All the time I'm focusing my mind on what I have to do, trying to eradicate my fears as far as I can.

I have a good idea with the gloves. I wring out my fingerless Millar mitts, which are soggy from belaying with wet ropes, squeezing them very hard to remove as much water as possible, and then put them on again. Then I put my big woollen Dachstein mittens over the top. This will save a lot of time when it comes to belaying, as all I'll have to do is take off my Dachsteins – which are dangerously slippery to belay with – and I'll already be wearing my Millar mitts underneath, with their superb grip. Having two layers of gloves also means that my hands will be warm and cosy, even when I've got them on the ice. What with my Dachstein mitts and my gaiters on, I'm feeling almost comfortable now in this godforsaken chasm that has all the geniality of a tomb.

I get to my feet. John, too, is completely ready, lashed to his belay nuts in textbook fashion, with the ropes already around his waist in the correct belay position. I'm completely psychologically prepared, and it's now just a matter of getting on with it, and getting this *mauvais pas* behind us as quickly as possible. But we mustn't rush it. It'll need a very "softly, softly" approach. I must simply go very carefully, and keep in perfect balance … not that my balance has ever been particularly good.

… Ooh, I say … here they come! … dumb, dumb, dumb … plainly bonkers … shuffling coils of hangmans nooses … slings and hammers flouting fortune … swinging ice-picks … singing swansongs … Ha, ha, ha! … Ha, ha, ha! …

At this very moment another couple of rocks about the size of footballs go whining and whizzing past, like perfectly timed warning shots from the Great Troll. Gee whiz! Bombs of schist from the Troll's barbican. Forbidding entry.

John says nothing. I say nothing. There's dead silence again, except for that constant background burble of disapproval:

Ha, ha, ha! … Think they can do it? … What silly plonkers! … Ha, ha, ha!…

Ignore it, Gordon! It's just a question of mind over matter now. Really: *you can do this. This is your finest hour … England expects …* Etcetera.

I look at my watch. The hands have been wrenched around again, all the way to … I can't believe it! … *Ten to nine in the evening!* As if the sick-humoured Trolls have got right in amongst the cogwheels of time itself.

8.55 pm

I'm perched once again on the preliminary holds below the first steep ice bulge, all ready for what amounts to my second big "entrance exam" of the day – though the first one is already such a distant memory that it could have been a week ago. I'm trying not to think too much about what I've let myself in for, but I'm under no illusions that this is going to be anything less than the most demanding piece of climbing I've ever done in my life. Not because of any great technical difficulty, but because of the very real and obvious dangers.

It's all going to be down to the style I do it in. This is the secret of all climbing, really. Climbing safely has nothing to do with simply "getting up", but all to do with seeing just how well you can do it. Style is your safety net, and it gives you confidence. When faced with a very serious pitch, you must always start from the conviction that you *will* get up it. There can be no room for any doubts. Once you start having doubts you are finished. In effect, you've already failed. Once your confidence goes, your safety net is removed, and it's all down to what little security is offered by the rope – which, here, is very little indeed. All the rope can do now is stop me going all the way to the bottom of the mountain, three thousand feet below. It can't stop me injuring myself very badly if I fall off.

I've already decided on a new, unusually rigorous strategy. Just as neatly and as carefully as I possibly can, I'm going to cut every single step – every single handhold and foothold. Tempting as it is, I'm going to refrain from kicking a single step. The ice is just too fragile, shatters far too easily, to risk that.

And I'm going to have to think very carefully about exactly where I'm going to cut the holds, the exact line I'm going to take. As far as possible, I'll climb in a series of slight zigzags, so that the holds are not in a straight line with one directly above another. The ice crust will remain much stronger if they are offset. If they're in a straight line, and the ice breaks, the whole lot could collapse, like tearing one of those double-perforated paper strips down the side of a Jiffy Bag.

Above me, to my right – though I can't quite see it yet – lies the centre of the gully, where the angle sets right back; so my plan is to cross this initial ice-wall diagonally rightwards to reach it.

Even the first foothold is problematic. If I place it too high, that'll mean putting too much strain on the handholds. If I place it too low, too close to the one below it, that'll make the ice skin dangerously weak. I've got to get it just right, first time. There is absolutely no room for trial and error with such a fragile surface. I've just got to make one clean set of perfect holes in what amounts to a pristine sheet of the most delicate porcelain. Just so many holds as I need, and exactly where I need them.

So: very carefully, holding the ice axe quite lightly in my right hand, I cut a neat little step just to the right of my right knee. Then, holding the top of the axe like a dagger again, I stick the pick into the ice crust to the right of my head, in one positive movement, as if I'm putting my fist down very decisively on a bare table top – no fiddling about with it once it's in – and, using it as a handhold, step up, smoothly, gently, but confidently. No dithering; just expressing my faith in myself and in nature – showing that we're in this together, my own nature and Mother Nature working together as one.

All my weight is now being taken by the thin blade of ice under the instep of my right boot. Don't even think about it. Cut another handhold; then, very delicately, using the ice axe now with my left hand, cut another foothold just left of my left knee – and bring my left foot up into that.

John is very silent.

This is really crazy: I'm now fully established on a nearly vertical bulge of delicate ice, with virtually all my weight being taken by two quarter-inch wide wafers of ice under the insteps of my boots. The compressed sugar-snow under my toes is taking a little bit of the weight, but really it's just the glistening, crispy crust that's holding me. I smile to myself, even though there's rather a bitter taste in my mouth. Really this bears little resemblance to any conventional kind of ice climbing. It's more like climbing up a curtain of egg shells, or a very delicate ladder made of bones and feathers, scarcely strong enough to take my body weight. And all on my insteps! It's absolutely crazy!

Yet, in accomplishing these first moves successfully – the opening gambit in a chess-game of climbing that I have to win – I begin to enjoy the challenge and the seriousness of it. Emotionally, the best climbing is always an almost exactly equal blend of fear and thrill … and the thrill is coming through now very stongly, surging through my bloodstream. This is ADVENTURE spelt with capital letters, and it's intoxicating. It's scary as hell, but very satisfying at the same time. I know I'm doing something very foolhardy, but I'm doing it with expertise.

The secret is total concentration. I can't see anything now except for the wall of blistered, crystallised snow-ice directly in front of my face. There's no room at all in my head for anything but the technical details in front of me, no room at all for any thoughts about the sucking vacuum behind and below me. This is unquestionably one of the most dangerous situations I've ever been in, one of the maddest things I've ever done, but I think I can master it.

No: I *know* I can. I know, therefore I can.

As I start cutting my next footholds and handholds diagonally rightwards, I start talking to myself. Just keep it very methodical, nothing rushed, one step at a time. But don't dither; try to keep up some kind of flow. "Unhurried speed" is the term the great French alpinist Gaston Rébuffat uses. If you dither for a moment you'll just get scared shitless, and maybe grind to a halt, unable to move up or down. Then you're finished. Just keep up some kind of momentum. Trust what you can do. Dispel all doubts. *Just keep going*. Far from being daunted by it, try to enjoy it. As Rébuffat says, "the joy of climbing well" is all about getting to know the substance of the mountain like an artist or a craftsman. It's a very special relationship. You have to get to know all its secrets, its good and bad qualities, just like a person. Yes, that French geezer was dead right: it's a bit like a conversation. Like a very unusual conversation with Nature.

It also helps me in my new-found role of "ice expert" to give John a running commentary, explaining what you have to do:

"You've got to be really light on your feet. Treat it really delicately … Really spread your weight." I'm talking straight to the ice slope in front of me. I can't look round. Just like talking to a passenger when you're driving. You have to keep your eyes unwaveringly on the road ahead.

"Does it feel quite strong?"

"Yeah, it's surprising. It's stronger than you'd think. But you must never kick. You've got to place your feet very carefully." I'm careful not to indicate just how precarious it really feels. Because it goes without saying just how careful John's got to be when he comes to second it. This is not the sort of territory where one can even *contemplate* a slip – so obvious are the dangers. Of course, if the ice does break when he's seconding, it won't be nearly so serious because I'll be holding him from above on a very tight rope.

So, I just keep going up my ladder of ice crystals – with, all the time, this little voice telling me: Yes, this may be the most dangerous thing you've ever done, but you're in control, you're mastering it …

It might have taken me five minutes, it might have taken me twenty, but in what seems like a moment – a very long moment suspended in this strange Troll world with its peculiar Troll time – I find myself looking over the top of the ice bulge, straight up the gully, which cleaves its way towards the jagged skyline like a great, gloomy, white-floored corridor, tipped at a crazy angle.

I carefully cut a nine-inch long foothold on the edge of the snow slope to my right, whack the pick of my ice axe into the slope above and right of my right ear, and step out and up, perhaps rather too confidently. But the ice holds me, and immediately I'm standing in a much friendlier situation with the slope set back to about forty-five degrees, maybe even less – but I still feel very lonely indeed, poised on an absurdly insecure apron of rotting ice. Nevertheless, a new wave of excitement sweeps over me. *We can do this!*

I look down at John's upturned, anxious face. "Hey, I tell you what, this is alright! It's actually quite fun – believe it or not!" Again, saying it out loud, even if it's not strictly true, helps me a lot.

But my optimism soon fades when I look at the sides of the gully – and see that the edge of the snow has melted even further away here on either side. So I cannot reach the rock at all safely. The edge of the snow is far too fragile, and this means – something that I've half expected and braced myself for all along – that I'm not going to be able to get any pegs or nuts in the rock, anywhere on this whole horrendously dangerous pitch.

A long way above me, high on the left-hand side of the gully, there appears to be a small bay where the angle sets back slightly, so that is what I'm aiming for now.

Very slowly, one step at a time, with the thin lines of my ropes trailing away behind me like vapour trails of fear – unattached to anything, emphasising my extreme vulnerability – I make my way on all fours, as it were, in humble obeisance, up the great tilted corridor of the Mountain King. My head bowed to the ice, not daring to look up. A little persistent insect on a very strange pilgrimage to the sanctuary of the Great Peak of the Trolls. To put it more bluntly: I'm really in the lap of the Trolls …

John's voice is calling up now from very far below, warning me that I'm running out of rope. The ledge I'm heading for is only about fifteen feet above me. I mustn't pause. If I break my great ladder of eggshells, I'll plunge three hundred feet down the gully to almost certain death. And if I can't find suitable belays on this ledge, we're going to be in very serious trouble indeed. But don't think like that. Just get to the ledge.

Then I'm there, very precariously. Chopping down the top of the snow beneath the rock ledge with my ice axe to make a step. Suspending the ice axe from my wrist and getting my hands on the rock. Stepping up onto the ridiculously fragile ice step. At which moment, the worst possible moment, I feel the full one hundred and fifty feet of rope come tight on my waist, preventing me from straightening up, putting more strain on the foothold; and John, very far away, calling:

"That's it – that's your lot!"

"I'm safe now!" I shout, lying desperately. "Can you untie your belay to give me a bit more rope?"

This is definitely the most dangerous thing I've ever done in my life.

"Are you really safe?"

"Yes!" I'm not just an "expert ice climber" now, I'm a reckless liar with it.

"OK … Hang on! …"

That's what I'm doing, John!

The rope slackens at last, and I grovel onto the gritty sloping ledge, wrapping my arms round a huge rock bollard with a rounded top, heart pounding. But the rope is absolutely drum tight on my waist again, so it's a hell of a strain on my arms. With one hand I get my biggest tape sling off from around my neck, drape it round the bollard, and clip the krab directly into my waistband. The tape is not very far below the back of the bollard, but it'll do. Just.

"OK, John, I'm safe!"

Liar. That's my own voice – that ridiculously cheery public announcement echoing down the corridor of the Trolls. He's probably wondering why I said it a second time … wasn't I meant to be safe already? I haven't even got my story right; so I add:

" – Can you move up a bit, because I want to get on another

belay." Trying to sound calm, that's half of the job.

The rope slackens again slightly, and I can stand up straight at last. We're now both attached to the mountain by a single paltry piece of nylon tape, looped around a sloping knuckle of rock. I'm breathing quickly; that used a lot of adrenaline.

The crack at the back of the bollard is a bit flared, but there's a narrowing that's sure to take a peg. I select a nice, meaty half-inch "angle" – a chromoly-steel piton that has a V-shaped cross-section, a bit like a crudely fashioned kitchen implement for removing apple cores – and whack it down into the crack as hard as I can with my peg hammer. Let the Trolls know who's master!

And what a good sound it is! One of the most beautiful pieces of music I've ever heard. Ping – ping – ping, ping! *Ping! PING! Absolutely perfect!* You could hang a double-decker bus from that … well, maybe a small family saloon car …

What are you talking about, Gordon? You're babbling.

I suddenly feel quite faint, and very cold. I've passed my entrance exam with flying colours, but I used a huge amount of nervous energy on that pitch. My blood sugar is obviously very low; in fact I'm running on empty now. I really must have at least two or three squares of our precious chocolate the moment John gets to me.

I turn round very wearily, facing outwards, to see the full, colossal drama of the situation that I'm in for the first time. I'm pinioned like a tiny insect specimen in a giant black slot with a white base and near-vertical walls on either side. There's cloud below – *where's that come from?* – and the great four-thousand-foot-high turret of the Romsdalshorn opposite me looks more grimly sombre than ever. But, deep down, as I take off my Dachstein mitts, exactly as planned, I'm feeling quite pleased with myself, pleased with a job well done. I stuff the damp Dachsteins very carefully into my anorak pockets under my cagoule, its underside already dripping with cold condensation, and take some very deep, calming breaths.

Then I hear the giggling water again, louder than ever. It's now a veritable stream of sarcasm:

… bungling stumblers blowing bubbles … shooting lines of far-fetched fables …

wobbling toddlers wanting water … short of chocolate … Ha, ha, ha! …

I interrupt angrily: "Taking in!" and start to haul in the ropes as fast as I can, ignoring the cackling babble from below. John has been very patient, and must be as cold as an iceberg by now. We've got to keep the show on the road, a two-man team of travelling players on an icy pilgrimage.

The ropes come tight and "That's me!" comes straight back, distantly, from the depths. I flick the ropes right back over my sack, so that they end up nestled around my waist, and call down into the void:

"Climb when you're – "

"*– Climbing!*" No farting about. John's climbing immediately. At first there are a few jerky, hesitant rope movements, and then it starts to come in steadily and smoothly through my mitts as I take it in around my waist. There's a pause. Good heavens, he can't be resting at the top of the first ice bulge already, can he? Then I feel the ropes go slack and, gosh yes, he's moving again. Yes, he must be past the bulge. My goodness, he's moving fast! And very smoothly. He's obviously climbing as fast as he can.

He comes into view, about a hundred and twenty feet below me, confirming my speculations: a little dark blue beetle on the white snow slope, scuttling very purposefully up towards me as if climbing a ladder. Which he is, in a way: a ladder of gossamer rungs, with a three-thousand-foot drop beneath him. Without the security of an ice axe, he's simply using the spike on his peg hammer to steady himself, relying mostly on balance.

When he arrives at my stance, he's very out of breath, but I can see he's impressed.

"God almighty," he says, "that was scary!"

That's all he says. He's gazing up at the gully above – where there's the promise of hundreds of feet of the same – not letting any emotions show. Just a faint frown.

About an hour later

I'm now nearing the top of the third rope length that we've climbed in the gully. It's another "unprotected run-out", with about a hundred and twenty feet of rope dropping heavily from my waist in the half-light, unattached to anything until it reaches my brother, hidden in the inky black cleft on the left side of the gully somewhere far beneath me. But it's going well, no doubt about it – in fact, in some ways it's going rather better than we dared hope, despite the seriousness of it. We're making good progress: we've climbed over four hundred feet up this delicate filigree of ice in little over an hour and a half, and I'm very much in control of the situation. I've got the technique completely taped now, so that it's settled down more or less into a routine. Not far above me – maybe as little as a hundred feet – the angle appears to drop back slightly, so we're nearly past the worst of it, and "all our trials, Lord, will soon be over"! It's just a matter of keeping my cool now, keeping going very steadily, picking my way, step by custom-made step, up into the gloom.

But in the last few minutes there's been a slight change – a change so subtle that at first I scarcely notice it, or choose to ignore it because it seems of such little consequence.

The angle is increasing ... surreptitiously, insidiously ...

And now, as I look up, I can detect it visually. I hadn't noticed it before in the twilight, but now I can see clearly that the slope is rearing up in front of me, slightly concave. And I can feel it under my toes and fingers as I teeter up on my punctured skin of brittle glacier mints, more aware than ever of the weight of the sack on my back, the drag of the ropes, and the pull of the void beneath me. It's extraordinary how one moment an ice slope can feel OK, and the next, a lot less than OK – how just a few degrees can make all the difference between it feeling acceptable and very dangerous indeed. I've edged almost unconsciously leftwards, as I vaguely start to consider the possibility of finding a belay in the left-hand rock wall, forlorn as it is. But there's absolutely nothing obvious yet: it's all very slimy and ice-polished, completely smooth, with no cracks at all.

I call down: "How much rope have I got left?"

Pause.

"Only about twenty-five to thirty feet, maybe a bit more."

Gosh, surely I haven't run out that much already?

"Are you sure?"

"Yes, about thirty feet max!"

I'm now only about eighteen inches from the fragile left edge of the snow that here curls up in a delicate fin of ice, more an *objet d'art* than a solid mountain feature. But I'm not really looking at that, scary enough as it is – I'm looking at what lies beyond, on the other side of it. At the gap between it and the rock wall. It's huge, about two or three feet wide. Unlike the last two pitches, where I could reach the gully wall quite easily where I belayed, here I'm totally cut off from it. With this delicate fin of snow-ice in the way, there is absolutely no possibility of reaching the rock; and even if I could, it appears to be entirely devoid of cracks or holds of any kind.

I glance across at the right-hand side of the gully – now about twenty-five feet away – and see that the snow has shrunk even further from the vertical rock wall on that side. I am, in effect, completely cut off from the rock on either side, poised on a broad white ribbon of precarious snow-ice that may or may not be very securely attached to anything.

My temples pulse hotly under the headband of my helmet as the full implications of what I can see sink in. The last five or six climbing moves that I've made have been on very thin ice indeed, and there is no way that I can reverse them safely to look for a belay lower down. I have been concentrating so much on the climbing, and so little on the question of belaying, that I've got myself into a very serious predicament indeed. With an escalating sense of horror, I realize that I have no chance of finding a conventional rock belay before I run out of rope. Unfortunately, there is absolutely no alternative but to use that very old-fashioned contrivance known as an "ice-axe belay". It's never crossed my mind that this might be necessary in this gully – that this is what we might have been letting ourselves in for.

My only consolation is that I have learned all about making ice axe belays on my recent Glencoe winter climbing course. But like a bad dream, my twin brother's clairvoyant voice wafts up from far below:

"Is there a problem?"

I clear my throat. It's very dry. *Make it sound trivial.*

"I can't get to the rock," I shout – "so I'll use an ice-axe belay!"

A momentary pause at this unwelcome news.

"Are you sure it'll be OK?"

"Yes, it'll be fine."

I can feel my heart pounding. *Just keep very calm, Gordon.*

I look up to the right where the gully widens out into a steep, fan-shaped bowl. It's obviously going to be best to get as near as I can to the centre, where the ice-skin is likely to be at its thickest and strongest. But I can't go much more than about fifteen feet, because I'll need quite a lot of spare rope to construct the ice-axe belay with.

As I move slowly rightwards towards the centre of the gully, cutting one careful step at a time, as methodically as ever – ever further from the reassuring proximity of the left-hand gully wall – I feel lonelier than I've ever felt in my life. But, very soon, and much to my relief, I find that the ice does indeed become a little thicker, and progressively more secure under my feet. In a matter of a few minutes I find myself looking into a slight hollow at shoulder level, providing an obvious place to belay. And, glancing up, I see that I am even closer than I expected to the point where the angle of the gully begins to ease off. It can't be much more than twenty feet above me, and about twenty or thirty feet above that the slope sets right back and curves out of sight. In a few minutes it's obviously going to get a lot easier, and safer. I feel a wave of relief and elation. *We've bloody nearly cracked it!* Wow!

OK, steady, Gordon! Don't count your chickens before they're hatched; but it's looking good. Time to report to John.

I shout: "I'm there! … I just need to make a ledge!"

"OK," comes distant reassurance.

My first task is to cut a platform that I can stand on.

Balancing carefully on my insteps, on the last two biscuit-thin ice holds, I cut a huge hole with my ice axe in the glinting depression in front of my face. Then I thrust my gloved hands deep into the cold marshmallow interior, ramming the snow downwards as hard as I can with my forearms while being very sure to keep my body as still as possible so as not to put undue strain on my footholds. I keep cutting the bottom edge of ice down with my ice axe as I do so, until very soon I have constructed a "ledge" of snow about a fifteen inches wide, at thigh level. Very carefully, I bring my left foot up onto it and put some weight on it. It creaks down a few inches, and then a lot more as I increase the weight. Then it stops. Now I dagger my pick into the ice above and right of the ice scoop – and, very gently, using it to help shift all my weight over onto my foot, I bring my other foot up onto the ledge. It sinks down a long way, maybe nine inches, then stops. The snow ledge is holding me.

Now I start to shift around on my feet to let the snow bed down still further, and the surprising thing is just how well it's holding me. In fact it feels very much like standing on an ordinary rock ledge that's covered with a thick layer of snow. I can start to relax a bit for the first time in at least half an hour.

It's important to work out a strategy for the belay before I start to construct it. One advantage of using a double rope is that it provides two separate anchor points, so I can use one for the ice axe and the other for a snow bollard. The first thing to do is to construct the snow bollard, because I need the ice axe to make it with.

Anyone who doesn't know about these things might think that a snow bollard is a bit of a farce, but my experience in Glencoe has taught me otherwise. I've made quite a few of them, and know just how remarkably secure they can be. Anyhow, having two separate anchors conforms with the old maxim, "Always use two belays where one will do." Every little bit of extra safety counts.

So, first, with the pick of the ice axe, I scratch a big upside-down U-shape in the rough surface of the ice above the ledge, about two feet in diameter, sketching out the outline of the bollard. I'll have to admit it feels more like an artistic exercise than a serious mountaineering technique, but – what the hell! – this whole enterprise is feeling quite bonkers enough already.

Keep smiling, Gordon!

What you do next is – tap, tap, tap – you make a semicircle of perforations with the pick around the line you've scratched, then very carefully start to cut a slot. Gently does it, don't rush. Real craft, this; I know John's waiting, but this is serious stuff. Even if it *is* vaguely reminiscent of building sandcastles.

Once I've gouged out the slot in the snow with the adze of the ice axe, I very carefully scoop out the loose snow with my Dachstein-mitted hand. It showers down onto my boots.

Gosh, that looks neat! What a work of art this snow mushroom is! It really should be on public display somewhere, and not left up here, hidden from view in this very private place…. I wonder just how long it will stay here after we've gone, before it melts away, unappreciated and neglected?

"OK, John!" I call. "Give me tons of slack on yellow! Just belay me on red!"

"What?"

"Belay me on red! – Give me slack on yellow."

"OK."

I make a huge loop in the yellow rope and lift it up around my newly fashioned snow bollard, carefully nestling it in place, sliding it around a bit like a slow bandsaw, feeling it dig in under the mushroom cap. I pull the loop so that it comes tight on my waist, and put some tension on it. Yes, amazingly, it's already offering some resistance. And I know, from Glencoe, that very soon it'll freeze up and solidify, and should soon be able to hold my full weight.

I tie the free end of the yellow rope back into my waist krab with a good old-fashioned "round turn and two half hitches", and then lean out, putting some weight on it. Wowee, that feels good! It's really holding me. Yes, you gotta smile.

Now the ice-axe belay. This is still what it's all down to, really.

"OK, John, give me slack on red!"

"OK!"

" – Won't be long!" God, I think I'd rather be up here, stuck in this really exposed position in the middle of nowhere, with something to do, than just waiting down there in John's truly horrible black slot. Just waiting and trusting that I know what I'm doing.

I put a clove hitch in the red rope, and slip it around the shaft of my axe, sliding it up until it's under the pick. Then, holding the axe very firmly, with both hands round the clove hitch at the top of the shaft, I reach up as high as I can with the shaft pointing straight down, looking for all the world as if I am about to drive a wooden stake into the Troll King's heart.

I aim very carefully – I've got to do it in one decisive movement – and drive it vertically downwards in one forceful thrust, right up to the hilt – all fourteen inches of it. It goes in alarmingly easily, without so much as a sigh; yet, when I wobble the top slightly, and put some tension on it, it feels surprisingly, reassuringly, firm. What I can't do is wiggle it any further to test it. That would only weaken it. I just have to trust it; but I know from my experience in Glencoe just how effective an ice-axe belay can be, and this feels like a surprisingly good one.

"How's it going?"

"Fine! – It's going to be just fine!"

"It's getting bloody cold down here!"

"I know … I won't be long!"

The top of the ice axe shaft is actually sticking out slightly where I was holding it, which is just as well, because it gives me access to the clove hitch, which I can now adjust so that the rope comes tight on my waist. I tie it in, just like the other rope, and lean on it … and – my God, that feels firm! Really solid. This has to be one of the very best belays I've ever constructed! Talk about shipshape! I'm feeling a bit tired now – well, very tired really, but pretty pleased with myself. I know I've done a really good job here, so there's no harm in feeling a little bit proud of it, surely? This is *real* mountaineering. My goodness, I've learnt a lot in the last year or two! We've come of age, really. All our carefully learned skills, honed in the Alps and Snowdonia, have really come together here.

I flick the ropes triumphantly over my back, right over my sack – I've become rather adept at this now – so that they end up around my waist, resting above the belay krab on my waist band. And then I take off my Dachstein mitts and put them in my pockets, so that I'm holding the ropes in my "slip-resisting" Millar mitts. (A great system this! I'll always use it in future.) Good. But … hang on a minute, Gordon! If John gets into trouble, and needs a tight rope – or slips (heaven forbid!) – it's going to impose too direct a strain on these classic old snow anchors, however good they are. I can go one better. Here is a perfect case for using a "shoulder belay", where the upper half of my body can act as a kind of shock absorber, so that the strain on the belay is reduced to a minimum if anything goes wrong.

I carefully unpeel the ropes from around me, and reposition them round my upper back, the rope from John coming up under my right arm, then across the top of my back, above the shoulder straps of my rucksack, and down past the left-hand side of my neck through my gloved left hand. I pull up my anorak hood, and then my cagoule hood, so that the rope is running snuggly round them next to my neck.

Perfect! It's hard to imagine how I can improve on it now. I'm standing in an absolutely classical "shoulder belay" posture, with two state-of-the-art snow belays. Facing out, and slightly rightwards. My right hand has the "live" rope to John, which then goes up across the top of my sack and over my left shoulder, while my left hand holds the "dead" end at about chest level. My right hand is pointing straight down the ropes in approximately the line that John will be climbing. It's the very model of a snow belay, fit for any mountaineering manual. Rébuffat or Blackshaw, I dare say, would give it full marks. It *looks* good, anyway. Remember that splendid old adage used in the aircraft industry? "If it looks right, it'll fly right!"

"What in the hell are you doing, Gordon? – What's going on?"

"I'm nearly there, don't worry! Just checking it!"

Keep calm. Have I really got this completely right? Yes, the "dead" rope from my left hand will pile up neatly between my left boot and the slope as I take it in. It's never a good idea to let it dangle in a festoon beneath your belay ledge. It's always better to keep all the dead rope up on the belay ledge with you. I'll be taking in the rope in such a way that it'll dangle in neat loops around the side of my left foot.

OK.

"Climb when you're ready!"

My confident command rings out in the gully, the voice of the proficient mountaineer who knows exactly what he's doing. Then there's silence, deep silence, and I realize for the first time that I can no longer hear any running water. No carping commentary, as if the excellence of my belay has silenced all possible criticism. I am completely alone with my thoughts. And for the first time, I can really absorb the full drama of the situation we're in. It's really stupendous. I'm looking straight down a spectacular fairground slide with a difference – this one being about twenty feet wide and four or five hundred feet high, and set between two huge, vertical black rock walls. At the bottom it curls over into the clouds, and what I know to be a near-vertical two-thousand-foot drop to the screes. It's a really tremendous image, like something out of a movie – it would make a great Panavision shot, this great gash in the mountainside with the clouds below (I have fantasies about getting into the film industry one day).

The truth, however, is that I've never been in any place that's been remotely as lonely, or scary, before.

Pud – pud – pud – pung – pung!

The distant sound of John's peg hammer snaps me out of my day dream as he removes his peg belay, emphasizing a sense of teamwork (a "well-regulated ballet" I think is the expression

Rébuffat uses). Then there's silence again. He's undoing his belay knots, organizing his gear.

I quickly get my watch out of my pocket. My gosh, tempus fugit! *It's a quarter to midnight!* Absolutely crazy. Troll time.

Cool it, Gordon! Just don't be surprised by anything anymore on this route. This is the nature of it. It's a little bit more than we were expecting. OK? But really it's just fine. Just keep a grip on yourself!

"Climbing!"

"OK!"

About 11.50 pm

Gosh, I'm feeling weary! I hardly slept last night, I was so keyed up with excitement, and now we've been climbing more or less non-stop for over eighteen hours. But I'm feeling quietly satisfied, despite the extreme seriousness of what we've been doing. For one thing, I'll have to admit I'm feeling a teeny-weensy bit proud that my hunch about the gully has proved so correct. It's been dangerous, sure, but not very difficult; and now we're nearly past the worst of it. As soon as we get back onto the proper route, we'll find a nice bivvy ledge where we can snatch some sleep before climbing the last relatively short section to the summit in the morning. With a bit of luck we'll be at Stegfoss in time for breakfast.

I can see the little dark speck of John moving out onto the luminous whiteness of the snow far below me, then he starts to come steadily, silently, towards me up my line of steps. Of course, I can't see the steps from here in the semi-darkness, but I know he'll be impressed. They're a pretty neat job by any standards. As Rébuffat says, "to leave a good-looking line of steps is like leaving one's signature on one's work."

John's climbing surprisingly fast considering he's been standing in one place for over an hour. In fact, I reckon he's going faster than ever. And the ropes are piling up neatly against my left leg, as I take them in, just as I've planned.

What was it that Rébuffat said? This is my favourite bit – it really needs a French accent to do it properly! " … Then, while his movements follow one another in smooth succession, the climber is aware of a quiet satisfaction as if he were receiving a silent approval" … How does it go? … *"In such a way does spring water, born of ze earth, flow gently, embracing ze banks!"*

I really must look that up again when I get home. Come to think of it, I haven't seen that book lately. What's it called? "On Snow and Rock", I think. Maybe Dad's borrowed it … I'll have to get it back from him when I get h——

Instant of doom –

— John is falling, shooting down the slope.

There's no transition, no warning at all. Just two images. First: the little dark figure of John, about forty feet below me, coming steadily up the concave slope. Next: he's shooting downwards at a fantastic speed – a little bundle in a puff of spray.

And without a sound. Just two silent images, fixed in time, for all time.

The rope inexplicably slack in my hands.

Shocking fact.

A second later

An almighty jerk, and the ropes are ripped through my fingerless Millar mitts with extraordinary violence, as if at least three people are tied on the end of it.

My left hand is slammed up against my chin as I clench at the rope, and my bare fingers are thrown open by the heat. The rope's going too fast and sears my fingertips like a red-hot poker as I try to clench it. I just can't do it with my fingerless mitts; the fingers just won't shut; each time I try they're flung open by my reflexes.

Impossible – gone – the rope is whipping through my fingers, slipping through my palms like quicksilver – completely out of control. Lost it! In a fraction of a second, I've lost it.

The dark speck that was John is hurtling down the gully out of sight with amazing acceleration. If I fail to hold him – and the belay gives way when the rope runs out – we will both be falling together – with my ice axe trailing uselessly on the belay rope behind me. And we'll go to the bottom of the mountain.

I *have* to stop it, or we're finished. Dead.

I put all my strength into trying to remain upright, trying to slow the rope with my hands. The great weight, the hurtling mass of John's body is twisting me round – *twisting* me – *twisting me* – pulling me down. Wrenching me down and round to my right.

It's as if my brother is falling through empty space, and I'm trying to stop him with my bare fingers clutching at a red-hot cable.

The rope is whining round the back of my neck like a band-saw – now such an absurdly short length on my slippery cagoule that there's virtually no friction – and I can feel the heat coming through the anorak hood next to my skin as the rope digs into my neck.

The stance must hold. It *must* hold, or we're finished.

I'm bending my legs to reduce the strain on the snow ledge, but my upper body is being twisted right round clockwise with the weight – twisting my chest towards the slope as I'm dragged down and sideways by the great weight. My feet sinking into the snow, my heart sinking towards hell.

The snow ledge suddenly collapses, and I'm lying on my side on the slope, suspended from the ice axe, my right cheek against the cold snow-ice, the whining rope thrashing uncontrollably around me like a living thing –

Ice axe must hold! –

– rope racing round the back of my neck at terminal velocity now –

Or we're dead.

The angry snake of the rope is snatched from my mitts and, as if I've been grabbed by a gigantic hand, I am hurled outwards into space.

And now there's nothing but air, and buttresses coming at me at a crazy angle.

So this is death. This is it.

I have only one thought:

What will people say? It's all I'm concerned about.

And with it comes the strongest, most putrid, most horrible emotion I've ever experienced in my life. At the very end of my life. It's absolutely sickly and disgusting, overwhelming everything, even the shock of what's happening to me:

The shame, the immense shame.

We've let the side down – we've let everyone down – particularly Dad. *How bloody, bloody stupid!* How utterly disgusting, how truly pathetic.

The *shame.*

I bounce heavily on the snow-ice, and then I'm flung out into the air again, very far out.

… And now we'll just become a ghastly taboo subject, only ever to be mentioned in hushed tones – if at all – wiped from history, too awful ever to be discussed. A subject to be passed over as quickly as possible. *"The Stainforth twins"* – now merely a label for something quite unmentionable, a phrase reeking of the unspeakably shameful.

How bloody, bloody STUPID!

All this, and more, passes through my mind as I plunge to my death.

I begin counting the bounces as one counts the seconds in a dentist's chair before being gassed. But this will be for eternity.

It's not unpleasant.

"Two!"

Another heavy impact, and I'm catapulted into space again.

"Those tragic Stainforth twins who went and killed themselves in Norway. Who let their father down!"

The sad, pathetic, unspeakably stupid *"Stainforth* twins"! Now posthumous.

"Three!"

The mountain slams into me with all the violence of a car crash, and is frozen static as in a freeze frame, as if I've driven into a wall of rock. A mighty impact without pain. No feeling at all; everything reduced to just one simple, hard physical fact.

Rock hard. Stuck fast. Head first. Fixed in time. Pinned like an insect.

I am just an observer. Looking straight down the white snow of the same awful gully, curving away below me with the clouds beyond.

Nothing else at all.

Perhaps this is what it is to be dead?

I can see my little steps coming over the first ice bulge – twenty, thirty feet below me – then nothing but clouds. No sign of life. No ropes. Nothing. The rope's gone.

Then – worse than anything I've ever experienced – worse by a long way even than dying – the most terrible realization hits me harder than any rock buttress –

John's gone!

– my heart ripped out –

John's gone.

This is the worst moment in my life – if in fact I am still alive.

John's gone.

And now I'm just left up here to die, very slowly. Hanging head first four thousand feet up a mountain in Norway. Just stuck up here for ever, for just as long as it takes for me to die.

I wish I'd gone with him. Can anything be worst than this?

No. This is the end of life, the end of everything. I'd be much better off dead, not just left up here on my own to die.

Now I'm moving, somehow, squirming round, using a sharpish edge of rock beside me, trying to turn round, trying to get upright. At last I'm crouching on one knee, on a sloping rock ledge, gazing down at the clouds in a complete daze – the full horror of it sinking in, wondering what in the hell to do.

Just what in the hell do I do? Now John's gone? – I'm in hell, after all.

Very faint, almost as if I've imagined it, a voice in my head. My name. As if from very far away.

My head jerks round in astonishment, to look over my right shoulder.

The great white, black-walled chasm roars up into space above me, hemmed in by huge rock walls, totally unclimbable. Just this ghastly white corridor of the Great Mountain King, tipped at a crazy angle.

And right in the middle of the corridor, about thirty feet above me:

John's head.

Just his head, resting in the snow. That's John's head.

Where's the rest of him?

I'm very scared. What to say?

"Are you alive?" I ask fearfully, tentatively, incredulously. There's a real possibility that John is dead.

"Yes, I'm fine" – the head speaks – the voice very peculiar in tone. Then immediately, "Are you OK? Are you injured?" – rather faint and nervous. But it's John's voice alright.

He's alive.

I'm alive.

"… *I'm alive!* …" I blurt in answer.

Why does he think I'm injured?

I'm clutching my knee, trying to stand up. I don't know why.

I *have* to get to my feet, have to get all my weight on my right foot. I can't.

What's holding me?

"Don't move! Don't move!" John's voice is very firm and calm, not shouting. But very urgent: "Just stay exactly where you are … !"

I realize that most of my weight is being held precariously by a cat's cradle of ropes going up towards John's head …

"I'm alive … I'm alive!"

I'm babbling it over and over again like a baby, trying to stand up, trying to extract myself from the ropes. Clutching my left knee.

"Don't move – just stay exactly where you are! I'll belay you."

"I'm alive! … I'm alive! …" I'm still struggling to believe it, truly astonished to be back in the land of the living with John.

I'm on both feet now, hobbling around, rubbing my knee. Then

I realize just how little is holding me, suspended on a sloping shelf of rock about a yard wide, nearly flush with the snow. There's a rope caught round my right leg, and there's a rope coming to my waist. But it's not clear exactly what's holding me.

"Don't move! Just stay there. Try and get belayed."

All the time, almost without realizing it, I'm rubbing my left knee very, very hard, the pain at first a detail. But, in the moment I notice it, it's as if someone has got hold of a huge lever of pain, and is pushing it up and up, beyond all limits, higher than one would believe possible. After about twenty seconds, it's almost unbearable.

Surely the pain will ease? No, it doesn't. I just have to keep rubbing. I rub so hard I'll probably have no knee left in a minute.

… *Got to get a belay on, got to get a belay on* … Chattering now.

The back of the ledge sticks up in a small spike. I get my biggest sling off my neck, drop it around it, and clip myself onto it, kneeling on my undamaged right knee. I now realize that the "ledge" is obviously the top of a large chockstone that's jammed in the gully, its top protruding from the snow. I don't remember noticing it at any point when I climbed up here earlier.

John's doing things with the ropes – hauling, throwing. A loop comes down to me.

"Get this round you!"

I take my sack off, clip it to the sling, and get the rope round my waist. It's what's known technically as a "belay". I'll tell you something about those one day.

Some time later

It may be a minute, it may be an hour, it may be a few seconds, I don't know. John is standing next to me with all the rope in a big pile on the boulder.

"Are you hurt?"

"I'm alive!"

He sees I'm clutching my knee.

"Is your knee alright?"

"I don't know – but I'm alive – I can't believe it! – I'm alive! – "

"I know you're alive! But what about your knee?"

"I don't know … "

I'm trying to speak, but I'm having trouble getting the words out. My mouth won't work properly, it's seizing up and wobbling. My jaws are starting to rattle. This is something else entirely new that I've never experienced.

And now something has got hold of my whole body and is shaking me, very violently, and it's not John. My arms are shaking, my head is shaking, my jaws are rattling, and my teeth are banging together like castanets. I'm become a stuttering machine, a back-firing old crock shaking itself to bits.

"… I think I've … probably bub bub … broken it … "

And now I start to cry – tears without emotion, tears of shock, tears of pain, tears of incredulity, tears of joy at being alive. Everything at once. All natural defence mechanisms gone.

"Sit down. Don't worry. It'll be alright."

How is John so calm?

I sit down on the ropes, a blubbing baby, my teeth clattering. I'm very, very cold.

"Aren't you hurt … at … at all?" I ask, my face wet with tears. Surely John must be hurt?

"No, nothing. I'm absolutely fine. Completely unscathed. I went into a very narrow crevasse. The soft snow absorbed all the shock."

"Haven't. Haven't you g-got any … bru … bruises? …"

"No, nothing, it's a miracle. I'm absolutely OK … Er, physically!"

All the time John is getting belays on, getting organized. It's astonishing. I notice, though, that his hands are trembling.

Now he's retrieving my ice axe, which is speared into the snow just to the left of the boulder, still attached to the red rope with the clove hitch – and he clips its lanyard securely to my sack. At least we've still got that. We'd be in even more trouble if we'd lost our only ice axe.

My injured knee is feeling very hot and restricted under my needlecord breeches, and is obviously already very swollen. I undo the adjustment strap, taking it right out of its buckle, and pull the breeches back so that I can assess the damage. It's a shocking sight. In place of my usual rather knobbly knee there's a huge, smooth, tight, shiny purple ball, that's throbbing and swelling almost visibly as I look at it.

I leave my breeches pulled back for the moment to reduce the pressure on it. I'll have to try bandaging it as soon as we've got ourselves better organized.

John has scooped away some snow from the back of the boulder, and has fed one rope round it as an extra belay. He gives me an extra sling to clip into. We now untangle the rope – this takes some time – and spread it out carefully on the boulder, backwards and forwards in loose coils, to form a makeshift mat for us to sit on for insulation. Just as we've seen it done in the textbooks. When we sit down on it, side by side, with our feet resting in the snow below the boulder, it's as uncomfortable as it looks. It's for all the world as if we're sitting on a sloping bench, the most extraordinarily situated bench we've ever sat on, with black walls of indeterminate height towering up on either side us of into the sky. It would probably be quite comfortable if we weren't sitting on a pile of rope. We each have our sacks beside us, attached to safety slings that are clipped into the belay rope. There are safety slings all over the place.

"By the way," says John, "what happened to the belay? I couldn't understand why you weren't holding me. It just felt as if I was falling through space, as if the rope had become detached in some way. Or broken, even."

I like that "*By the way*".

"I lost c-control of the rope with the fuf-fingerless mitts."

"But didn't you have a twist round your wrist?" He looks genuinely puzzled. "You don't need gloves if you're doing it properly."

"I m-m-made a m-mistake. I – used a – shou-shoulder buh-belay."

"You *what?* – You know they're crap!"

"I'm s-sorry … J-John! I thought – I thought it would … put – put less strain … on the b-b-belays. Which were – absolutely – u – useless … "

"So the belays failed?"

"Yes. They d-didn't do a th-thing. They offered no re-resistance at all."

I'm shivering, and my teeth are still chattering violently, but more with cold now than with shock.

"God, we're lucky!… You know, I saw this dark bundle flying over me just before I went into the crevasse – which must have been you. It's just bad luck you hit this boulder." He fumbles in his sack. "OK, we'd better have the last bit of chocolate."

He breaks the last piece of Fruit and Nut chocolate in half; just eight squares each. But as soon as I've swallowed it, I can feel the beneficial effects of even this small quantity of calories.

"And there's one sandwich left, but first we need to get warmer, and get better sheltered."

We decide to stay here for just as long as it takes to warm up, and for the shock to pass. If we're lucky we might be able to snatch an hour's sleep, but really we must move as soon as we can because my knee is obviously broken and is likely to get a lot worse. As it is, it's already seized up completely, locked solid now in more or less a right angle. This is clearly nature's amazing way of making a splint to immobilise it. And, as it's stiffened up, the pain has started to subside, and become duller and deeper as it's spread upwards into my thigh. It doesn't feel so bad now that I'm sitting, but the instant I put any weight on it, it's excruciating. That this is going to present a huge problem in terms of our survival goes without saying, which is why I'm not saying anything to John about it right now. We have more urgent matters to deal with first. We must try and get sheltered, try to warm up, at all costs.

Our sacks have inner waterproof sleeves made of very lightweight grey groundsheet material called "*pied d'elephants*" that can be pulled out to form long extensions. We slacken off our bootlaces and put our feet, with our boots still on, into our climbing sacks. The sacks have nothing left in them except our water-bottles and some spare hemp waistlines because we're already wearing all our spare clothing.

We pull the sleeves up, wriggling our legs into them, until they come all the way up to our hips. I immediately feel a lot warmer, almost cosy, but my face and upper body are still very cold. We're already wearing both our cagoules and anoraks over our Norwegian sweaters, so there's nothing else to add. But, exploring in the lid of my sack I find my old red woollen Swiss headband dating from my first days of climbing in Zermatt; so I take my helmet off and put the headband on to keep my ears warm, then put my helmet on again.

John, meanwhile, has got out the Space Blanket, which, frankly, we never thought we would ever have to use in anger, and is busy reading the instructions.

"'Warning: do not expose to direct flame. May burn if ignited'!"

"Oh, you don't say," I interject. "Don't most things b-burn when ignited? And why on earth w-would anyone want to ig-ignite it?"

"… 'Do not nick or puncture … Do not use as a ' – wait a minute! – 'do not use as a *tanning blanket*'!" – John's starting to laugh – "'Or *severe sunburn will result* … Full body wrap in worst weather may cause overheating'!"

"Oh, my God!" I say, "I h-hadn't thought of that! As if w-we haven't g-got enough to wer-worry about … we might s-start overheating!"

John's shaking his head in disbelief. "What do you think it says next?"

"I don't know. Go on … "

"'*Avoid contact with power sources or electric devices*'!"

"G-gosh – r-really?"

"OK, and there's one more thing … Any guesses?"

"No, h-h-haven't a c-clue!"

"'Not suitable for use with children or infants as suffocation hazards exist.'"

"Oh w-well, that rules us-s-out then, d-doesn't it?!"

This little piece of mirth has cheered us up no end; but not for long. John's got the Space Blanket out of its packet now, like a silver Mars Bar, and is unfolding it into a long snake about an inch and a quarter wide and over five feet long. The problem is it's very densely packed and all stuck together with static electricity. Almost as if it's stuck together with glue.

It takes us an extraordinary length of time, with our cold fingers, to unwrap the whole thing – our hands going systematically backwards and forwards, unpeeling each inch-and-a-quarter fold – until eventually, after perhaps twenty minutes or even half an hour (time means nothing any more), we've unfolded its full, six-foot length.

"What a fantastic palaver!" John says. "What a fantastic cheek to call it an 'emergency' blanket! It takes far too long to unravel it in a real emergency, particularly when you're in a state of shock. I'm going to write to them about it."

"You could r-r-write to our eM-p-P."

"I don't think he's particularly interested in mountaineering …"

We tuck the rustling silvered sheet of gossamer-thin plastic under our sacks on both sides to stop it flapping about in the breeze, because a chill draught is coming up the gully now. It just isn't wide enough to go over our heads; but at last we can get our hands into our sacks and put on our thick woollen Dachstein mitts again.

So now we're sitting like a couple of gnomes under a silver counterpane – rather like vagrants under the arches at the London Embankment. Only here we're uninvited guests in the middle of Valhalla, pretending to be ready for any trick the Troll King might care to pull next, but feeling very vulnerable indeed.

"OK, sandwich time!" John says. The very serious situation is that we have just one cheese sandwich left, plus a spare lump of cheese not much bigger than a matchbox. That's it. "We're going to have to ration it." John holds up the lump of cheese. "We'll keep this for the summit," he says.

Grand talk. "Summit?" The idea of reaching any "summit" now seems very fanciful indeed.

"I don't mean the top of the mountain," John says, "I mean the top of the route."

He turns to me with a haggard face, looking very serious.

"Because we can't go down, can we? ... Because we won't be able to get out of the gully. It looked well-nigh impossible to get any pegs in that ice-polished rock."

("Well-nigh" is another of John's favourite expressions.)

"And even if we could, we'll probably run out of pegs after just two or three abseils. Because most of the cracks need knifeblades."

"Yeah. And it would take f-far too long, any-w-way. It's b-bloody miles ... It's about f-four ... four thousand feet, isn't it? It w-would take us hours."

"Hmm!" John gives out an ironic sniff. "Pigs might fly! The whole thing's far too bloody dangerous. We'll almost certainly have another accident if we try and go down ... And we're much nearer the top anyway. So I'm afraid the only way is up! We've got to climb our way out."

We fall into silence for a moment, as the full impact of what lies ahead sinks in. The truth is, I'm rather relieved that John's so definite about it, because climbing up is certainly a lot more appealing to me with my painful, immobilised leg, than going down.

"It'll be m-much easier for me to c-climb up than d-down, anyway, with my knee. I c-can hardly b-bend it at all."

I take a bite of the cheese sandwich. It tastes remarkably good. It's the first proper food, I realize, apart from chocolate, that I've had for over a day. I eat it deliberately slowly; but John's finished his in a matter of seconds.

"How far do you think it is to the top?" he says.

"Umm ... I don't think it can be much more than ab-about eight or nine hundred feet above the point I got to."

"I doubt if it's even that far. I reckon it's only about six or seven hundred feet."

"Well, let's s-say seven to eight hundred to be on the s-safe side." I have the last bite of the sandwich.

"Do you really think your knee's going to be alright?"

"Well, it's going to have to be, isn't it? You're just going to have to do all the leading."

"I know. Don't worry." John nods his head up and down reassuringly. "It'll be fine. I'll give you a very tight rope if necessary."

"You're probably going to have to give me G sharp most of the time!"

"G sharp" is an old expression we use for a rope that's so tight you can play a note on it.

"By the way," I add, "you do realize that, not very far above where I got to, the angle sets right back? So it should get a lot easier."

"Yeah, and then we'll soon be back on the proper route."

It's the first time we've had a proper conversation for hours. But life is already completely different. Somehow it can never be the same as it was, ever again. All we can do now is look forward, not back, and try and survive. Because, if we look back for even a millisecond into that old life, we may not survive in this new one – this new world of mature "grown-ups" that we now find ourselves in, whether we like it or not.

We discuss reascending the gully and John lays down the law. We'll do it in very short pitches, stopping wherever we can find any sort of half-decent belay. We've got to try and find belays on the rock now, all the way, even if it takes much longer.

I smile sheepishly, "And waist belays all the way!…"

"Yeah, I doubt if you'll be making that mistake again!"

That's all John says about it. It's amazing. And he hasn't made a single further comment about my ice-axe belay, or even my very poor sense of judgement. Of course, he knows very well that a lot of what happens now depends on him. But it also depends on how well my knee holds up.

He concludes: "I think we should only stay here for about a couple of hours at the most, and get moving just as soon as we feel we're ready for it."

Oh my God. "Well, I need to get some rest first, because I'm still feeling pretty shaky. I need to get warmer, and try to get some sleep. The knee might be feeling a little better then."

Now that we have a plan of action we feel quite a lot happier about it. John starts stuffing snow into our water-bottles, while I turn my attention to my damaged knee, which I can hardly move now. My thigh is also starting to feel a little numb, and I'm worried that the numbness is spreading.

I remove my Dachstein mitts and get out the First Aid kit, which I haven't looked at very closely before. Although it's quite a small plastic container, there's a surprising amount in it: cotton wool in little blue packets, several bandages, a lot of Elastoplasts, a little tube of Savlon, and even some safety pins and a neat little pair of scissors.

I start by spreading some Savlon all over the hot, tight, bulbous dome of my knee, as if it'll do any good. But at least it feels pleasantly cool. Then I put a pad of cotton wool on top of it – it gives me confidence to pretend to know what I'm doing. (I'm quite good at that …) Then I start to wind a bandage around it in a complex zigzag pattern, and here I really haven't a clue what I'm doing. I finish the whole thing off with some safety pins, which makes it look quite professional, though I'd hesitate to call it a work of art. Now I discover a roll labelled "Adhesive Bandage". I unpeel it, and find it's really just a long Elastoplast without any of the padding, just a gluey fabric strip. So I wrap that round everything to help hold it all together. One big problem is that, with all the bandages and the swelling, the whole thing is now about the size of a small football. So, using the scissors, I make a little cut in the slit of the breeches above the adjustment strap; then, getting hold of both sides of it, I pull really hard, ripping the cloth open a few inches, so that I can get the breeches back over the knee without it exerting undue pressure.

John hands me back my water-bottle which, like his, he's now stuffed with snow. We put them in our sacks by our feet, hoping that our body temperature will warm them up, so that we'll be able to have something to drink before we set off.

I get my watch out of the left pocket of my breeches.

It says four minutes to midnight. *That can't be right.* Then I see that the second hand has stopped. I shake it. It's as dead as a dodo. That must have been the time when I hit the boulder.

I tell John. He gets his watch out of the lid of his sack. "It's quarter past one," he announces.

We put our Dachstein mitts on again, and pull the Space Blanket up to our necks. Then I get hunched in a foetal position with my arms wrapped round my legs and, although my breeches still feel very cold and damp except for the hot ball of pain around my knee, I feel a lot better now that we've got ourselves organized. By that I mean: a lot better in the context of the most serious situation I've ever been in. Really, I can't wait to get moving again and get out of this hell hole; because that's what it is, really.

Actually, on reflection, I think it should really be called "the Great Troll's Arse". (I'm thinking of the way the Peak Cavern in Derbyshire is called the Devil's Arse because of what the locals thought of the Norman warlord who lived in the castle directly above it.)

I shut my eyes, feeling a bit like a snail that's retreated into its shell, trying not to think too much about what lies above now, what lies ahead. The only sound is the rustling cellophane of the Space Blanket flapping about in the breeze.

II

MONDAY

Well, I've completely given up the idea of getting any sleep now. It's just not going to happen, because I'm far too cold – the much-trumpeted silver foil Space Blanket has proved to be absolutely useless – and my knee is just too painful. The rope is bloody uncomfortable to sit on, my left thigh is feeling quite numb, and there's a strange tingling sensation in my left foot. I try lifting it up and down within the cramped confines of my rucksack and wiggle my toes in my boots in the hope that improved circulation might ease the pain. But it doesn't. The throbbing, overinflated beach-ball that was once my knee has become a seething cauldron of complaint, and the bandage feels hot to the touch. The pain has subsided from its initial hot rage to a deep, subdued anger, but there's no knowing how it will react once I have to put any weight on it. Will this locus of rancour spread to an all-out rebellion of my whole body? Or will it simply remain an ever-deepening resentment, suspending its hour of reckoning to a later date?

My stomach, too, has complaints all of its own that go far beyond its craving for sustenance: tight knots of fear in anticipation of the very difficult day that lies ahead – which will surely be the most difficult I've ever experienced. If we don't pull this off, if my knee finally stops me, this could easily be the last day of my life. But I'm trying to shut these morbid thoughts out of my mind now and become a kind of psychological zombie, because today is going to be all about overcoming my fears, and showing a very "stiff upper lip", as my father would say.

So I'm admiring the view.

Which admittedly, in its very stern and wild way, is absolutely stupendous, the kind of mountain landscape I would normally be revelling in if I wasn't seeing it through such a strong filter of pain, and from a truly awful, diabolical viewpoint, in such a serious situation.

I'm gazing out of the ravine, with its near-vertical walls, at the dark flat-topped turret of the Romsdalshorn opposite us, with the twin-summited peak of Vengetind beyond it looking like a stately schooner in a sea of mountains that stretches to the eastern horizon possibly a hundred miles away. There is a dark ceiling of cloud moving slowly from right to left, but the sky above the horizon is clear and very bright, suggesting that sunrise can't be far away. It is, as the saying goes, a mountain landscape "to die for" ... well, I suppose that may be true for once. It's obvious that unless we get moving very soon we will be sitting here for ever.

And now I have a new thought. It comes on me very suddenly; and within a few seconds it's become a decision. Typically, with the more important ideas in life, it's hard to tell exactly when you have them. There is no protracted process, really, beyond a kind of vague initial mulling that's almost unconscious. It's as if they creep up on you stealthily and then grab you, taking you by surprise. When you make the decision you are emotionally already there, psychologically prepared for it. Well, that's what's happened to me now: I know what I have to do, and I have to tell John very soon.

John's hunched forward like a hermit, his eyes shut as if in prayer.

"John – are you awake?"

"Yes." He opens his eyes. "Wide awake."

"I don't know about you, but I'm bloody freezing."

"Yeah, really bad. This Space Blanket's absolutely useless. And every time I've felt myself nodding to sleep I've jerked forward onto the belay rope." He chuckles: "It's a sort of clever automatic system for keeping you awake ... Anyhow, how's the knee?"

"About the same. It certainly doesn't feel any worse. I really think we should get moving. There's no point in just sitting here getting cold, now that it's so light."

"Well, I'm glad you've said that, because I've just been waiting for you, really. If you're feeling ready now we should get going right away – because it's a case of the sooner the better, really."

"OK, let's get ready. What's the time?"

John rummages in his sack, and peers at his watch in the gloom.

"Five to two."

"God, is that all? That must be about the longest half hour I've spent in my life!"

I start rubbing my arms to get the circulation going.

"So you really think you're going to be OK with the knee?"

"I'm not sure – I hope so! I've got to be, haven't I?"

I take a deep breath.

"Actually, John, I've been thinking … I hope you agree …"

John looks at me furtively with raised eyebrows.

"… But I want to lead off."

John's eyes widen with surprise. "Really? Are you serious? Are you sure you'll be able to manage it with your knee?"

"Well, it's not going to make the slightest difference, really, is it, whether I'm leading or seconding. I mean on the snow, anyway. On the rock you'll definitely have to do all the leading. But I've really got to do this to get my confidence back. I mean just the first pitch or two, to get on top of it – psychologically – you know, like getting back on a horse …"

John can see that I mean it. "OK. Fine." That's all he says. No dispute of any kind. Great.

"But you must stop just as soon as you get to a decent belay," he adds. "It doesn't matter how short the pitches are. That's going to be the rule from now on. Bomber belays all the way!"

He begins to stir, with a great rustling of the silver Space Blanket. "OK, let's get moving!"

So the two very cold, vagrant snails, the hermit twins, now have to extract themselves from the relative shelter of the damp cocoons of their sacks and get ready to go on a pilgrimage, doing penance for their stupidity. (Well, my stupidity, mostly.) In my case it really is going to be a pilgrimage on my knees. Actually, I'm probably going to be climbing very much like a snail, come to think of it.

I hold on to the belay rope behind me to help me get out of my sack. This is the first big test, because I'm going to have to put some weight on my injured knee. First I extract my right leg from the sack and, pulling on the belay rope, get my full weight onto it, so that I'm in a crouched position on the boulder. Then, very carefully, I lift out my left leg, which is now completely locked in a right angle – well, at an angle of about a hundred degrees – and gently put some weight on it. Because I'm not going to be able to stand all day on one leg!

"Aghh!" My knee gives a hot burst of pain like a silent scream, forcing me to crouch forward as it fades away to a dull ache. Actually, it's not quite as bad as I expected, providing I don't try to straighten it. I've just got to keep it in this locked position. That's how I'm going to have to climb today, spending as much time as possible standing on my right foot, or resting on my right knee. Which is going to give me a very limited reach.

I'm also feeling very weak and groggy, but I mustn't show it.

John's folding up the Space Blanket.

I comment, "So much for the claim about ninety per cent reflectance!"

"I'm certain it's reflected precisely nothing. Not even one per cent!"

"It's scandalously bad in an emergency, isn't it? It's absolutely useless if there's any breeze at all." I rub my thighs and shins vigorously to get the circulation going.

"I suppose the idea is to get completely wrapped in it if you can. It then might just do something, but I doubt it."

"Willmott said it was big enough for two people!…"

"Well, it isn't. Anyway, I'm never going to bother with it again," he says, dropping it summarily into his sack, like dropping something rather unsavoury into a litter bin.

I get out my water-bottle, and I'm pleased to find that my body heat during the bivvy has melted quite a lot of the snow. So I can now have a much needed drink. It's got some granite dust in it, but it doesn't matter.

John says, "We'd better have the last of the cheese."

"I thought we were keeping it for 'the summit'."

"Forget that: we need the calories now, because we're cold."

Because this is the last of our food, we're going to have to climb for many hours with nothing else at all. It's a nice Norwegian cheese with quite a strong flavour, and it's surprisingly nourishing. It's also most definitely morale-boosting.

I take off my helmet, putting it carefully in my sack for a moment, then remove my headband, because I'll get too hot otherwise, once I'm climbing. Then I put my helmet on again. I'm "psyching up", as we say.

We quickly get the rope ready in the chill early morning light, separating it into two neat coils on the boulder. Then I put the big sling with the pegs on it over my shoulder, clip my four nuts into my waistbelt, and slide the peg hammer back into the holder on the side of my right leg. I start waving my arms about, rotating them in little circles like propellers, to loosen up and get the circulation going while John gets the belay ready.

Ah, one more thing – my bootlaces are not nearly tight enough, because I slackened them right off for the bivvy; and it's essential that my boots aren't swimming around on my feet. I crouch down and do them up really tight. One final thought: if I ever get off this climb alive, my boots will most certainly be going in the bin. That will be it. No more of this climbing malarkey!

I stand up again, and am astonished to see that John has the Leica out. What in the hell's he doing? At this of all moments? … He's taking a shot of the dawn, just like a tourist! And yes, it's certainly scenic, to put it mildly, because the first rays of the sun are now backlighting some of the wisps of cloud on the ridge of the Vengetind, transforming them into puffs of golden smoke.

Then, of course, on a moment's reflection, I realize why he's doing it. It's got nothing to do with art. He's simply doing it because he feels duty-bound to take a shot in case we never get out of here alive, and this will at least be a record that we were here – assuming our camera is ever found. So I say nothing; better just to let him take this picture for posterity.

A click; and he puts it away again without a word.

"OK, I'm ready," I say. "Time to get 'klatring' … 'Opp', as the Norwegians would say!" I try to sound cheery: "The only way is opp!"

"Well, I hope you're 'opp' to it!" John says drily.

Frankly, it's a relief to be getting started again, and to be leaving this hell-hole of a bivvy spot. At least we're going to give it our best shot. If we're going to die, at least we're going to die fighting – well trying, anyway. Actually, I once had a real classic of a school report when I was in the Lower Fourth Form, a real stinker – I promise you I'm not making it up: "All that can be said of him is that he's been trying. Very." That's exactly what it said …

I'm standing on the edge of the boulder, with the steps that I cut in the snow last night just a couple of feet to my left, exactly as I left them. It's strange that I don't have any recollection of seeing this boulder last night, I suppose because it was flush with the snow and I was concentrating a hundred per cent on cutting the steps.

"OK, watch me," I say rather curtly.

"Good luck … Don't do anything I wouldn't do!" John has put on a hopeful grin, thankfully.

I whack my ice axe into the crust, and make a long step left with my injured leg, putting it carefully into the left-hand of the two steps closest to me. I pull on the ice axe and rock my weight over onto my left foot. Just as I feared, there is another very sharp burst of pain, as if someone has stuck a hot needle under my kneecap. But, hey! I'm going to have to get used to this now for many hours to come. It's simply a new fact of life I've got to put up with. All that matters is that I get up this bloody mountain at all costs, however painful. And providing I don't try to bend my leg, it really isn't quite as bad as I was expecting: because as soon as I've done the manoeuvre, the pain reverts to its previous dull throb. Just keep it in that right-angle, that's what it's telling me. And the good news is that the rest of my leg is still working fine, although my thigh is very stiff. Just try and spread the load, and keep the weight on the left leg to a minimum.

I've also made another very encouraging discovery.

"Tell you what, I think it's frozen up a bit. It definitely feels a bit more solid than last night."

"That's good," John says.

This discovery gives me an unexpected boost of confidence, and I quickly step up to the next foothold. Yes, it definitely feels more secure. Another good point is that, without having to cut any steps, I can keep moving and build up a rhythm. It's just like climbing a rather rickety ladder. Also, I don't have to keep my weight on my left leg for any length of time. If I want to rest I simply shift my weight onto my right foot.

But I'm equally aware that I mustn't rush it. I need to take it as gently as possible because one false, careless move – bashing or twisting my knee – could spell disaster.

"You know, I think this is going to be OK," I call down.

About a quarter of an hour later

There are some things in life you have to do, that give you no choice, otherwise you'll die. It happened to me last summer in Llanberis Pass when I was making my first Extremely Severe lead – well, the guidebook gives it "Extremely Severe, but only just" – a slightly overhanging V-shaped groove about seventy-five feet high called "Brant Direct". "A pitch to delight the connoisseur," it said. "With patience and strong fingers adequate protection can be arranged." Well, the trouble was, not being a connoisseur, I found it very difficult to get on any protection. It was just so sustained, and there were no proper resting places. After about fifty feet I could feel my strength going; I had only got on a couple of runners, and there was a real risk now that if I fell off I would hit the deck. There was a shallow spike in front of me, and with great difficulty I managed to get a tape sling over it. By this time my big toes were almost bursting under the strain of bridging out on the minute holds, so I had to move up very quickly. There was a whirring sound, and John called up, "Your runner's off!" "I know," I said, trying to sound calm. I looked up, and saw the top only about twenty feet above me. I just said to myself, "You've got to get up there", and the incredible thing was I seemed to float up it in a kind of trance – well, some people might call it a blind panic! – and the next thing I knew I was looking over the top at this sloping ledge. At this point I relaxed slightly, thinking, Phew, I've done it! Only to find that the final move onto the ledge was really precarious and difficult. I had well over thirty feet of rope out now, dropping away from my waist, so if I came off I was definitely going to deck it. The problem is that, when you're exhausted, your footwork goes to pot. I don't know why, but it just does. I could feel my toe starting to slip, so I muscled up on my arms using every last ounce of energy I could muster. I don't know how I did it, but I did. Basically, because I *had* to.

Well, the same's happened this morning. I've just climbed seventy or eighty feet up this very steep rotten snow in my badly injured condition, and I'm not quite sure how I've managed it. But here

I am, back at the very same first belay in the gully that I used last night, using the very same angle peg, and sitting on the very same rock flake to take the strain off my knee. Who would have guessed that I'd ever be back here? … I just hope it's the last time.

"Well done," says John when he gets to me.

I ask John about the crevasse. It looked incredibly narrow when I passed it.

"Actually, it's quite a bit wider than it looks, under the surface. You know, I went right into it – several feet under.… I'd heaved myself up a bit by the time you saw me."

"No, I didn't realize that."

"It was quite extraordinary. I was so surprised to suddenly find myself in there, completely at rest and in the dark. I couldn't really tell if there was anything under my feet. The amazing thing was that I was completely unhurt, because God knows what speed I was going when I went into it."

"So you really haven't got any bruises?"

"Well, just one very minor one on my right hip, but it's not affecting my climbing in any way."

"I'm not feeling too bad either. Not as bad as I was expecting. So, do you mind if I carry on for a bit?" I'm still much keener to put myself in this strong position of leading. It's doing me a power of good psychologically.

"No, fine."

About an hour later

We've now climbed three shortish pitches from the bivvy boulder, varying in length between about seventy and a hundred feet. We've been climbing like complete automatons, with all our emotions, if not completely switched off, pushed to one side as irrelevant. It has all passed in a blur of determination. We are totally focussed. We have scarcely spoken a word. The only sounds have been the chimes of the peg hammer pinging off the huge side walls.

I've managed to construct a good belay in the crack between

the snow and the rock of the left wall at the top of the third pitch, just below the steep section where it all went so horribly wrong last night. Near the beginning of this pitch I passed a distinct scoop in the icy surface of the snow, a strange dent, like a bash in the side of an egg shell. Obviously that's where my first bounce was.

"OK, I think it's time now for me to take over," John says when he reaches me.

I'm only too happy to hand over the lead. I've restored my nerve, and feel that to some extent I've redeemed myself. I can see that John's rather keen for me *not* to lead the next pitch. I suppose because it would be a bit like tempting fate. He's probably also thinking there's a risk I might be tempted to use an ice-axe belay again, or something. As a twin, of course, I can read his mind perfectly.

So I give him the ice axe, holding it sideways in both hands with my arms extended, as if I'm presenting him with a special gift. It's very precious, this talisman of all our hopes, this key to our survival. It might as well be the Golden Bough. In return, I take his peg hammer, which he thrusts at me with considerably less formality. With its ridiculous little spike. (No wonder he fell off climbing with that!) It certainly doesn't deserve any pomp or ceremony.

John wastes no time and sets straight off, keen to get it over with, it seems – and knowing that, from where I'm belayed, he will be able to reach easier ground at the top of this pitch. But he's not taking any chances. Just below the scene of his fall, visible as a great pear-shaped hole in the surface ice, he manages, rather boldly, to lean across the fragile left edge of the snow and get a peg in the rock wall for a running belay. Ping – ping – ping – *ping – ping!* It really is a most reassuring sound at this point. Then, without further ado, he makes some new steps to the left of the hole, and in a matter of minutes he's following my previous steps, and making it look for all the world as if he's walking up stairs. The myth of his alleged inferiority at climbing on snow and ice is dispelled with few brandishes of his ice axe. Very soon he's casually calling down that he's passing the scene of my ice-axe belay … 'Quite a mess!' is his only comment … and now he's cutting steps and breaking a new trail, as it were. True, this slows him down a bit, but the rope goes out steadily through my mitts as he disappears from sight over the crest of the steep section. And astonishingly, within about five or ten minutes, I hear the peg hammer ringing out again. Perhaps it's another runner?

"OK, Gordon," comes the cheerful call, "I'm belaying here at a good rock ledge!" And a few seconds later:

"Taking in!"

I'm so happy that for a few minutes – until I start climbing again – I forget all about the pain in my knee. But once I start climbing, even though I'm seconding now, I have to take it just as slowly and carefully as before. Normally, in climbing, you don't give your second a tight rope unless he asks for it, but now John's keeping it very tight indeed, almost winching me in the manner of an Alpine guide. When I get near the scene of my fall – which I can see out of the corner of my eye as a huge churned up mélange of loose snow to my right – I make a point of keeping my attention fixed firmly on John's neatly cut line of steps in front of my face.

When I reach him, sitting happily on a palatial ledge, it's a hugely important psychological moment. I simply say: *"Non deficit alter!"* and manage to affect a grin.

John knows exactly what I mean, of course, because it's our family motto. *"He did not fail a second time."* At least that's one interpretation of it.

All he says is: "Have you noticed the sun?"

"No." I look round. The sun is now backlighting a large smoke-like puffball of cloud lying between us and the Vengetind, slightly below our level. The sun itself is obviously just about to appear from behind the near-vertical buttress which blocks off the left side of our view out of the gully. What is particularly encouraging is that, although there are bands of cloud, there's a lot of clear sky in the distance. The improving outlook comes as a kind of visual endorsement of our upbeat mood.

John quickly gets the Leica out again and takes another shot. I'm impressed that he's making the effort. It's all rather professional, as if he might write an article about it one day, or something ... if we manage to survive ...

"What's the time?" I ask.

"Four twenty-five."

"That's pretty good. We're doing well."

John is looking up the gully, which widens still further and curls out of sight to the left. We still have many hundreds of feet to go.

"You do realize", he says, "that we must now be just about opposite the high point we reached yesterday in the left-hand gully."

"My God, that seems a long time ago!"

"Snakes and ladders!" John says with a sardonic chuckle, and heads off again, kicking steps as he goes, because the angle of the snow is now so benign that there really isn't any need to cut steps any longer.

Another hour later

We've been in the sun for quite a while now, and although I can't remember ever having been quite so happy to feel its warmth when it first reached us, the gully has just gone on and on, and I'm now quite hot and sweaty. My knee isn't liking the heat either, and the pain has spread further up into my thigh. It's a very dull pain, but it means I'm still having to climb very slowly and carefully. On this easier angled snow-ice I'm in effect on my hands and knees; and one advantage of this is that it's keeping my damaged knee quite cool, and acting as a kind of local anaesthetic. I'm also continually biting my lip, to help distract my attention from the pain. With John out of sight above, I'm completely lost in a world of my own, and just wondering when this nightmare will ever end. Or if it ever will.

And now we've run into an unexpected obstacle. I look up and see that the snow runs out, and that John's belayed below a steep rock-band about forty or fifty feet high. It's not the angle that's the problem, but the fact that it looks very smooth. And is it so much as mentioned in the guidebook? Of course not.

A new thought has come to me now – I don't quite know where it's come from – that the real route doesn't come up this "main gully" at all, and never has done. That virtually no one, except perhaps Tom Patey and his team on their winter attempt nine years ago, has ever actually been up here.

When I reach John, I get clipped into his very substantial belay, and off he goes. He just walks up it, making it look incredibly easy.

"What's it like?" I ask as he gets near the top.

"Oh, about Mild Severe, not too bad! The rock's very rough."

Umm. Mild Severe is actually quite hard; as I soon find out when I come to second it. My big problem now is that I can't stand properly in balance because of the knee – in fact, I'm having to rest on it, and it's agony. Apart from which, climbing slabs on your knees is not the way to do it. Instead of climbing properly, with conventional slab-climbing techniques, I'm having to press my fingers into the smallest rugosities and claw my way up it while John winches me on the rope.

There's a harder move which I have to do with a bit of a bounce, and there's a shooting pain in my knee. "Ouch! Tighter!" I scream, and John hauls.

When I reach him I realize it's taken a lot out of me, and there are tears in my eyes. But it's a great relief to get to the top of it, and find that we're back on the snow again.

Without any warning at all, there's an almighty crack like gunfire, high above us.

I cringe. There's no time to look up. That's a classic mistake to make, anyway: how to get a rock in your face! Better for them to bounce off your helmet. So I keep my head tipped very slightly forward, and hear the missiles whirring down behind me. There is silence for a moment, then a stupendous cannonade as the rock fragments ricochet down the gully, bouncing off the walls hundreds of feet below, where the ravine curves to the right and narrows. Probably at about exactly the point where we bivvied, I reflect grimly.

"My God!" says John. "That was much bigger than the ones last night."

"It must be the sun getting onto the face."

"Yes – that would have been our lot if it had happened any earlier. This gully really is bloody dangerous."

There's a vague hint in his tone that it's my fault … Which it is, really.

I comment, "God, can you smell that?"

"Yes, that's cordite …" Then impatiently, "We really must try to get out of here as soon as possible."

"You don't say."

5.50 am

My heart gives a little leap of fear – *That looks impossible!*

I've come over a slight bulge in the snow-ice to find John sitting about forty feet above me in a dark corner below a huge chockstone blocking the head of the gully. The slabby left-hand retaining wall isn't very high now – perhaps no more than about sixty or seventy feet – but it's repulsively smooth and slimy; while the right wall, glowing yellow-orange in the early morning sun, is pretty nearly vertical. The chockstone above John's head is fringed with huge icicles. It's an impressive spot.

"Where does the route go?" I ask in alarm. Is it possible that at the very moment we thought we were going to escape from the gully, we find ourselves trapped in a cul de sac?

John doesn't seem too bothered. "Oh, I'm sure there's a way!"

When I reach him, sitting in his sunny alcove, I find that he's got his plastic water-bottle cleverly perched in the snow in such a way as to catch the drips coming from one of the icicles. This looks like a good idea, so I get out my own water-bottle and do the same with another drip.

"I've been looking at this wall," John says, "and I think there's a way I can get up there and traverse back above the chockstone."

At first glance it looks very unlikely, and then I see what he means. There's a system of narrow broken ledges on the right wall, and if he can get established up there he may be able to traverse back to the top of the snow-capped chockstone, which looks temptingly close. The tantalising question is: What happens above the chockstone? How close to the col of Ugla Skar are we? Is it just a few hundred feet, or have we still got a long way to go? I've no idea, and the mountain is giving away no secrets yet.

Fortunately John's suggested route turns out to be a lot easier than I expected, and he's soon about fifteen feet up the wall and traversing back along a narrow ledge, brushing off the snow as he goes. He even manages to get a good runner round a flake to protect me on the traverse. Then he's directly above me on the chockstone, and wet snow is showering down on me and the pile of rope. (The ropes are getting ever wetter from the water dripping on them from the icicles.)

"What's it like? Can you see anything yet?"

"I can't quite tell … but it looks quite easy … " He's keeping me in suspense.

He disappears from sight, and the rope continues to move out steadily.

"Can't you see anything yet?"

"Not really, but I'm on good rock now … I should be able to get a belay on in a minute … "

What does he mean, *Not really?* Why's he keeping me in suspense?

"Are you out of the gully?"

"Yes."

Then why's he not telling me what he can see?

Another pause, and then just what I want to hear:

"Taking in! – ging in!"

Ah! Our old friend, the echo, is back!

"That's me!" I am just overjoyed to be getting out of this ghastly gully at last.

"Climb when you're ready – you're ready!"

"Climbing." "OK – K."

In my enthusiasm I waste no time in getting to grips with the rock. It's quite rotten, there are a lot of loose flakes, but very soon I'm at the traverse line. There's a lovely incut edge where John's cleared out the snow, and good footholds. Hey! This is almost fun, dare I say it? My spirits have soared. Soon I'm stepping carefully left onto the top of the chockstone where again John has cleared away a lot of snow. I make a few awkward moves up and can see him silhouetted against the sky on the left, sitting on a slabby rib. I just can't wait to get up there. At last we have escaped from the bowels of Store Trolltind, this latrine of Valhalla that I have grown so thoroughly to detest over the last nine hours. And my hands are sinking into the most reassuring holds I've come across so far on the entire route.

"Great rock!" I exclaim.

"You haven't looked up," John points out much more soberly.

Oh my God! Moving out onto the rib I can at last see the rest of the route. We have come out of the gully into a vast rock amphitheatre. It must be seven hundred feet across, with the towering summits of Brudgommen and Store Trolltind framing it on either side, and Ugla Skar, with its very distinctive guardian "Owl", still an incomprehensible height above us. Far, far further away than I'd either feared or imagined.

Plus, it all looks very steep indeed.

"It's a bit of a downer, isn't it?" says John when I get to him.

Funny way of putting it. Yes, well, we are a long way below the top. It looks like thousands of feet. We have monumentally misjudged how far up, or rather, down, the route we are.

"God, it looks a long way …" I give a huge sigh, weary yet philosophical.

"What do you reckon?"

"It may not be quite as far as it looks." I'm clutching at straws. "It could be a bit of an optical illusion. I mean, perhaps it's only about six or seven hundred feet … "

John's face is a mask of scepticism. He shakes his head. "No, I don't think so. I reckon it's at least twelve hundred." That downward-sloping mouth is John at his most serious. He's not going to let any wild fantasy get in the way of scientific fact. He's also no doubt thinking just how huge a weight of responsibility he now has in getting me up this route in my injured state. I don't know what I can do to dispel his gloom. But the truth is I'm not feeling quite so downhearted myself now that I've looked at it for a bit. Yes, it looks a long way, and quite steep, but the rock looks good, even quite friendly in the sun. And, really, all that matters to me now is that we are alive, and that we've got out of that horrible, horrible gully.

Fortunately, John's mood suddenly changes. "OK," he says breezily, "On we go!" and gives a little sigh.

We are on a huge, steeply shelving sheet of slabs leading up to some kind of a terrace below a steeper rock wall. John heads up towards the terrace making it look like a Sunday afternoon stroll. OK, a Monday morning stroll, in fact. Like he's on his way to work, and has been this way a thousand times before.

You've got to keep your spirits up, Gordon, or we're doomed. And, when I come to second the pitch, I find the answer. Just *sing*. It's made a lot easier by the fact that we're suddenly on the most unexpectedly good rock: rough, dry and firm, and covered with good holds. It's by far the most friendly stuff we've encountered on the whole route so far. Nice, nice gneiss. If only we'd had some of this a bit earlier! I'm also thinking just how lucky we've been, really. How John just happened to go into that freak crevasse when we fell – because we've passed nothing else like it in the whole gully this morning. And also the way the snow froze up a bit last night. That was a nice surprise. So I start humming *Hey Jude*. I'm never going to be able to hear it again now without remembering the strong Norwegian accents of the guys singing it on the ferry when we came over ten days ago. "De, da da, da-da-da da! … da-da-da da!…"

My God, this is amazing rock!

8.10 am

I'm in a fantastic position now, limping along the bottom edge of a steep bank of snow, in effect a balcony running across the face, with the huge pillar of Brudgommen plunging down ahead of me, and the verdant floor of Romsdal spread out, map-like, four thousand feet below. It's scarcely possible to imagine a grander mountain situation. It would not be unfitting to call this a "Traverse of the Gods" – sorry, of the Trolls. Although the sky is overcast now, and the valley floor has become quite dark, there are one or two sun patches further up the valley that only add to the "sublime" drama.

It took us two full pitches to reach what we thought would be a terrace, only to discover this rather large snowfield that we couldn't see from below. John reckons that this may in fact be the relatively small "speck" of snow in the final couloir that we spotted on Saturday night from our tent. If he's right, it confirms that we still have a long way to go. But, like the rock rib we've just climbed out of the gully, this snow gallery is proving remarkably straightforward, even friendly. In fact, things have been going so well for the last hour or two that I'm starting to think that there's a vague chance we'll get up this horrible route, after all.

I'm actually leading again now because, being a horizontal traverse, it really doesn't make much difference whether one is leading or seconding; and we've saved time by not having to change over the belay. Also, it's a way of keeping up twinly morale by giving a sense of teamwork, however misleading it is, seeing that John has been virtually hauling me up the route. Plus, it gives him a chance to have a bit of a rest from doing all the route-finding. Not that there's any problem with finding the route now: there's literally only one way we can go. The top of the snowfield, about a hundred and fifty feet above me on my right, is backed by a huge near-vertical rock wall; but ahead of me there are some rocky ribs leading up towards what appears to be some kind of deep chimney-crack. Nothing else on either side of the crack looks remotely climbable at Grade IV. So that has to be where the route goes.

Of course, leading means that I'm having to break the trail again. But actually it's not as bad as I was expecting because the sun has obviously been on this snow for many hours, and the ice crust here is so thin that it offers very little resistance. My bent knee forces me to adopt a most peculiar crouching position, limping along with my left foot on the very bottom edge of the snow, while my right leg scrunches through the deeper snow on my right. Because of the nature of the slope, I'm forced to turn towards it in a very novice-like way, in order to take as much weight as I can on my good, right leg, and my ridiculously short ice axe. I could really do with Whymper's alpenstock now! But it's a Catch-22 situation, because taking my weight on my right leg means that my left foot is forced to lead the way, and it's very painful every time I shuffle my weight forward onto it.

In this peculiar bunched-up position I'm also getting a close-up view of my damaged knee; I can see now that there's a large dark patch of congealed blood on my breeches. But I'm damned if I'm going to look at it any time soon. It's definitely a case now of the better the devil you don't know. Strangely enough, I find that speed helps, so once I've mastered the special technique required, I scuttle along the lower edge of the snowfield like an injured crab, only interested in reaching some small rocks that I can see sticking out of the snow in the distance. Fortunately, I just manage to reach them before the full length of the rope runs out, and they provide not only a good belay, but a very comfortable seat that allows me to take the weight off my badly jarred knee.

When John comes to second the pitch, although it's little more than an easy walk for him, I notice just how carefully he takes it, because the ropes offer him absolutely no security. All he has to safeguard himself is his little foot-long ice-hammer; if he slips, he'll fall a hundred and fifty feet over the edge.

When he reaches me, all he says is, "Some position!" Then he takes the ice axe from me and leads on, kicking his way rapidly along the rim. There's no sense of any pleasure. Just a job to be done. As befits a Monday morning.

8.50 am

"Amazing this," I say as I stumble towards John, who's got himself lashed with multiple belays to a splendidly positioned perch at the end of the snowfield. "Who would ever guess from below, that this thing that looks like a little patch of snow is three hundred feet across? I remember it looking about sixty feet at the most from our camp site," I add, as I clip into the belays. "Two whole rope lengths! Amazing." I am really stunned by the scale of it.

"Um …" John answers vaguely, apparently only half listening. "There's something far more interesting than that …" He's looking down intently … "Take a look at that!"

"What?"

"What can you see?" in a rather schoolmasterly tone.

At first I don't see what he's looking at. And then – *Oh my God,* yes! It's glaringly obvious. Directly below us is the most incredibly friendly-looking, spiky ridge of rock, very much like an upscaled version of something on the East Face of Tryfan in Snowdonia. A bit steeper perhaps, but eminently climbable. It's so obvious it might as well have a big white dotted line painted up it.

"That's where we should have come," John says, putting the final nail in the coffin.

At a glance, we have final confirmation, it seems, that the proper route doesn't actually come up the main gully at all; that in fact it goes nowhere near it, and the guidebook description is thus completely wrong. Why, why, *why* didn't we find the correct route yesterday? It must somehow start in the region of that mysterious cairn where we fiddled about for so long, which we can't see from here because the ridge curls away out of sight. Still, there's no point in crying over spilt milk; it's all water under the bridge now … or, rather, fluid under my kneecap …

But John rubs salt into the wounds:

"I can virtually see the point where I must have been yesterday – I reckon I must have got to within about thirty feet of where it curls out of sight."

"Oh, come on, John – I don't think so!"

But he's going on, as only John can. "I had no idea it would connect up this easily! If only I'd known!…"

I protest that it could be steeper than it looks.

"Well, there was just one steep bit. I wish I'd forced it. *Look at it!* We would probably have been at this stance in about half an hour!'"

"Oh, come on, John! Don't be ridiculous."

"I'm not being ridiculous. It's a joke how easy it looks."

"But things always look easier looking down them, than looking up. Remember Lliwedd."

Anyhow, it's only of academic interest to us now. I am in a state of considerable anxiety, not to mention pain, and I'm really focused on the immediate task in hand, which is to get to the top. The good news is that we're definitely back on the correct route at last …

though it looks quite a bit scarier above, and not at all obvious. I'm still very anxious that my knee may worsen to the extent that I won't be able to get up the hard rock pitches that obviously lie ahead. I'm also anxious about the weather, because it's suddenly become very gloomy and there are ominous wisps of cloud drifting past the introductory slabs. I can't see Fiva Farm or our tent at all. It really doesn't look very healthy to me.

"Look John, we're on the proper route now. Let's just get on with it," and I tell him my worries.

"Well, where *is* the proper route? I've been looking around while I've been belaying, and it's not at all obvious where it goes." He gives an ironic smirk. "I suppose we'd better have another look at our old friend the guidebook!"

I get it out of the top of my sack, and read out the crucial sentence for the umpteenth time. That typewritten Courier text might as well be Egyptian hieroglypics for all the sense it makes:

"Da, de da, de da … *'moving right into the main gully and escaping by a hole and chimney* to Ugla Skar'."

"Well, let's hope this famous 'hole and chimney' is in that slot we can see up there." John's pointing at the chimney-crack I spotted earlier.

"It's just about got to be hasn't it?" I try to sound more hopeful than I inwardly feel.

"OK," says John, "we'd better put the ice axe away. We won't be needing it again for a while."

I strap it on to the special retaining straps on the back of my sack, while John puts some more snow in our water-bottles. "This may be the last source of water below the top," he says.

At least we're talking about the top now.

About half an hour later

We're in deep gloom, and getting worried. It's all started to feel a lot more serious again. John's belayed in an easy rock gully below a smooth slab leading up into a dark chimney slot that butts against the north wall of Brudgommen. As we've approached it, far from it looking more amenable, the more forbidding it's become. "Slot" is too tame a word for it. It's now grown into a mighty, cave-like chasm, topped by bristling overhangs. But we can't yet see into the back of it. The big question is: Will there be a way through? Is the notorious "hole" lurking in there somewhere? It's starting to seem very unlikely.

"I'll go up and have a look," John says. "OK?"

He goes up about another fifty feet, up nasty smooth, steeply shelving rock – what is technically described in geology textbooks as a "glacis". Then he stops.

"Hell – ell."

He's gazing up at it, motionless.

"Do you mean hole?" Trying to make a joke of it.

"No. There isn't one – isn't one!" John's voice rebounds off the wall of Brudgommen. "There's absolutely no way through, through. Come and have a look, look."

I'm starting to get very tired of that echo.

I stop about twenty feet below him. I can see enough. It's really bad. It couldn't be worse. I'm staring up into huge gloomy sentry box, perhaps a hundred and fifty feet high, with uniformly dark, grey walls of very compact rock, so featureless and smooth it looks as if it's been gouged out by a gigantic chisel. There's not a trace of even the narrowest crack at the back, let alone a chimney. Even if you could climb up the back by some extreme bridging, it's blocked off at the top by a huge horizontal overhang that ends with a savage downward-pointing spike, like a tooth.

It's an indescribably oppressive place, with everything that isn't vertical or overhanging, sloping. All leaning sideways to the left and dank and slimy, in various shades of green and black. Totally uncompromising. The overall effect is of a giant open coffin that's been deliberately placed in the back left-hand corner of the amphitheatre to bar all further progress.

It's a devastating blow. *To hell with the bloody "hole"!*

I'm not sure just how many more disappointments I can take.

And now, with spectacularly bad timing, just when things could hardly be worse, it starts to spot with rain. I only hope it's not going to turn wet. That's all we need now.

John is not so easily fazed. "It has to be out to the left," he reasons. "I can see a line of weakness."

I turn round. Out on the huge steep, slabby sidewall of Brudgommen I can just make out a vague groove line. It doesn't look particularly promising, but it's all there is on offer. So we decide to descend about a hundred feet to investigate.

I am feeling very despondent. Just when things had started to look so good, all the old doubts that cling like mist to this ancient, arcane route have come flooding back. The very walls drip with doubt, just as they start to drip with rain.

10.00 am

I'm sitting in the rain, enthroned on a rock ledge beside a snow patch, with the wet ropes around my waist, but without my cagoule on – with a bit of luck it's just a shower – while John gets to grips with his "line of weakness". Well, yes, it's a line of weakness alright, but what's peculiar about it is that there's no sign whatever that anyone's ever been this way. If this was a route in the Alps there'd at least be a peg or a sling or *something*; but there's absolutely nothing. (Come to think of it, just how many times has the Fiva Route ever been climbed? Maybe ten or a dozen times in thirty-eight years? Almost certainly no more. Possibly less.) Another problem with John's line is, yes, the first bit looks climbable, but then what? The wall just gets steeper and steeper. We have somehow got to get back into the main groove-line above the big cave – which I've already privately nicknamed "The Coffin" – but unless there's some kind of traverse line up there, this could well be a false trail that leaves us stranded in the middle of a blank wall. If so, we're in deep trouble. I don't ever recall having experienced this level of angst on a climb before – but then I've never been injured like this on a climb before.

Just pull yourself together, Gordon. If anybody can do it, John can.

He's slowed down a bit.

"What's it like?"

"It's OK." That's all he's going to say.

The rope inches out in little uncertain jerks, then much more rapidly. Then stops. I wait and wonder; and at last I hear the ascending musical scale of John's peg hammer ringing out like a tolling bell – Pong, Pong, Pong – Ping, *Ping!* – filling the ancient amphitheatre with a chorus of echoes. An impudent intruder in the fortress of the Trolls.

It falls on deaf ears. There is silence again. Then:

"Taking in! – taking in!"

"That's me! – me!"

"Climb when you're ready! – you're ready …"

God, that echo's getting on my nerves!

"Climbing! – bing."

Hope so! Now it's my turn.

The rain's stopped, but the rock is wet and glistening.

At first it's misleadingly straightforward, with unexpectedly good holds; but then it begins to steepen, and the holds get smaller, and soon it's a whole different kettle of fish. I've got a blank wall of rock in front of me with a narrow ledge at the top that I just can't reach. There's a very small sloping hold for my left foot which I can't use effectively because of my knee.

But I have to. "Give me some G sharp!" I scream at John, somewhere in the misty heights above me.

With John tugging and hauling like an Alpine guide with an incompetent novice, I step up onto the hold, trying to ignore the hot, sharp pain in my knee. I get my hands on the rounded ledge, and heave myself up with my right foot scrabbling against the smooth rock like an invalid trying to kick-start a motorbike. I manage to grab a higher hold with my left hand, pull up very strenuously, and eventually get stood on the ledge. Only to be confronted by another wall, similar to the first but with a much smaller ledge at the top that's even further out of reach. It's obviously going to be a lot harder.

Up to now, since the accident, although the climb's been long, tiring and painful, I haven't had too much trouble, technically, because I've in effect been crawling more or less on my hands and knees. But I can't crawl up a smooth, near-vertical wall. After a few attempts, I get my hands with difficulty onto the very sloping ledge at the top, and my right foot on the last usable foothold – but because my left leg is so bent I can't get enough purchase on the wall with my left foot to make any further upward progress … without using some very unconventional climbing techniques. There's nothing for it but to do what we call a "Harrison's Move" – at Harrison's Rocks south of London – which involves doing a very strenuous pull up and then swinging your leg right up to shoulder level, like a dog having a wee, in order to get it hooked on the same ledge that you're pulling up on.

The truth is that, as Harrison's Moves go, this is quite an easy one, but I've never had to do one before when I'm badly injured, and this is not at Harrison's Rocks, twenty feet above the ground in a romantic woodland setting in the Garden of England. There's nearly a mile of space below my feet, and my hands are grappling with rough gneiss that is very much less amenable than that gentle English sandstone.

I pull up very strenuously on the sloping holds, in effect dragging myself up as John hauls me, and swing my cocked leg up as far as it'll go, but I just can't get my knee onto the ledge. In desperation I'm bouncing it agonisingly up the rock. Somehow I have to get it onto the ledge. With John heaving as if he's trying to get a car out of a ditch, I give another bounce and get my knee hooked pain-scrunchingly on the edge of the ledge. It just so happens that it's not only unpleasantly sloping, it's also got a very sharp edge. There is such a thing as Sod's Law.

I reach up. Heck! There's nothing for the left hand. It scrabbles over the rock above the ledge trying to discover holds that my eyes already tell me aren't there – "piano playing" is the derisory term we use for this at Harrison's Rocks. I'm in an incredibly awkward position now, gasping prostrated like a beached whale, with my left leg lying sideways on the ledge, and my right foot trailing impotently on the wall below, while all my weight is being taken by the soggy ropes. I'm forced so far sideways that my head is almost touching the ledge – I'm almost eating it – while getting a close-up view of moss and lichen. All the time I'm pushing down as hard as I can with my right palm on the sloping ledge, while my right foot scrabbles ineffectively against the wall. Somehow I've got to get my weight onto my knee, however much damage it does – and then onto my left foot, however painful it is. I'm already starting to sag back – but John's not letting me. It's a spectacular demonstration of how not to do a mantelshelf move. The best thing I could do about it now is write a book called "I Chose to Climb Badly".

Actually, I have my own private mnemonic that helps me on the crux of a climb: *Look – Light – Laugh*. "Look" meaning, *really* look for all the potential holds – hidden undercuts or sidepulls, for example, as well as the obvious ones. "Light" meaning, use the holds with as light a touch as possible, like a cat on a hot tin roof. And "Laugh"? Well, it doesn't really mean laugh, it means stick a big grin on your face, however false (and however idiotic it looks), to at least *give the impression* that you're enjoying it. It's astonishing how this little trick often works for me. So, how's it working now?

"Light"? I'm like a sack of coal. "Look"? My eyes are on stalks of terror. "Laugh"? You must be joking.

"Take in! – *Take in!*" I screech at John, as if he can take the ropes in any tighter! He's literally *hauling* me, winding me in like a big-game fisherman.

I get my left hand on a small nodule, and John heaves like a navvy.

At last I've got most of my weight onto the tender punchball of my left knee. It's excruciating, as if I'm kneeling on a shelf of hot coals, but I'm winning, because I've now gained enough height to jump my left hand up to a better hold, and get the fingers of my right hand over a sharp crystalline flange – and so bring my right knee up onto the ledge next to my left.

So now I'm kneeling on the narrow ledge on both knees, but I'm not embarrassed; I'm really happy to be here at all, rather than toppling off backwards to dangle on the end of the rope like a puppet. Because all that's keeping me on the mountain now are these two drum-tight strands of red and yellow nylon. I grab them shamelessly, and quickly pull myself up and get stood on the ledge. I'm nearly in tears with the pain, but it doesn't matter, I'm on the ledge at last. And I'm in balance.

OK; now just keep going – you're probably past the crux. Just try to do it as fast as you can. Don't prolong the agony. Calm down. Try to take it easy, try to regain some composure. It's still very steep, but there are many more holds now.

And so, continually having to throw my left knee up sideways onto the holds and ledges, I carry on grovelling and graunching my way up towards John, trying as far as possible to ignore the shooting pain in my knee … until eventually he fields me, gasping and panting like a netted fish, onto his small and airy perch. He's effectively strapped into a small seat, which he's been using as his "game-chair" in his new-found role of big-game fisherman. Doing his Hemingway stuff. He's looking weary. The Old Man and the Fiva.

"Heavens to Murmagatroyd, that was hard!" I exclaim, as I heave myself aboard.

"It wasn't that bad surely?"

"I suppose not," I retort, clasping my knee – "if doing Harrison's Moves with your leg in a splint is your idea of fun!"

"Don't worry. You're doing fine!"

Oh, *Come off it, John!* I only just managed it. What if it gets any harder? Then we're really up shit creek without a paddle.

About ten minutes later, I think. I'm really losing track of the time

God, I hate this place! This great gloomy gulch, this vast, vertiginous headwall of Store Trolltind opposite me, the plunging pillars to its right, this preposterous scale, this crazy perspective, this precipitous verticality, this huge drop. I'm getting quite sick of it really. It's wearing me down.

Apart from anything else, I don't think I've ever been anywhere so utterly unaccommodating, so grotesquely alien, so grimly unsuitable for life. It's certainly not an environment suited to the rational animal known as man; it's a place surely fit only for raving lunatics … or complete idiots. Oh, to get back to the horizontal world of fields and flowers and human intercourse! I'm no longer the least bit interested in these petrified gargoyles, or granitic bridegrooms.

Brudgommen. The Bridegroom. Who would ever contemplate spending the rest of their life shackled to this cold, damp, cadaverous thing? It would be your classic "marriage made in hell", that's all I can say.

The rope has been moving out steadily, but now it's stopped, and we still have such a long way to go, it seems, in our role of insects in this Hall of the Mountain … *Shit Faces!* I nearly say it out loud.

"I'm there! … there." Oh, that bloody echo.

You may be there. But just where, exactly? Somewhere absolutely outrageous, I'm sure of that.

"Taking in! … in." *Taking in, taking in, taking in, taking in.* For ever. We're taking in all day, taking in all night…. We've been taken in all right! … By the Trolls. By these Norwegian shits.

"That's me! … me!" Is it? Is it me? I'm not sure what I am any more, except some kind of minion of these bloody Nordic Gods.

"Climb when you're ready! … ready."

Ready? Ready? I don't think I've ever been "ready" for nonsense as extreme as this…. Thinks: yes, I really should write a book about all this: "The Quest for Misadventure".

But John's tugging at me now to get started, to get on with it, encouraging me to take the bait, as it were…. By the way, the technical term for this in big-game fishing, in case you didn't know, is "trolling". Just thought I'd tell you that. Just what could be more appropriate? God, I'm so tired of it.

"Climbing! ... ing." *Trying to!* Well, pretending to. Pretending to be "a proper climber" rather than a complete "spastic" – as we used to call people at school who were total wimps … as I am now – with my hands patting the rock, my feet playing about, as all the time John keeps winching, reeling me in. Like a little cable car with bendy legs, scrabbling on the end of a couple of nylon strings – a floppy puppet filled with mush that used to be muscles. A right old bag – a mixed bag of pain and fear, doing "Harrison's" moves all the way, or pretending to – "Son of Harrison's" moves, "Grandsons of Harrison's" moves. Cocking my leg up, pissing like a dog, biting my lip all the time now to offset the pain in my knee that's bringing tears to my eyes. Tears? Oh God, don't be a baby. This is just so spastic! Grovelling and groping my way up the grey flanks of some stupid, pitiless "Bridegroom". *Clawing* my way up this manky shroud of schist. And … feeling very, very tired.

Actually, these comical, pitiful moves I'm doing are no more related to Harrison than I'm related to the Fat Face's Bridegroom.

I look up. John's head and shoulders are silhouetted against the sky. But what's this? What in the hell is this? "Joy through suffering", or something daft? – He's grinning like an idiot. Looking smug, even. What on earth, or in hell's name, is he so happy about?

He reads my mind. "Wait till you see this!" he says, beaming.
"What?"
"This ledge. It's amazing."
"What's so amazing about it?"
"Just wait and see!"

As I get closer to him, I see that he's sitting on something that looks very much like a garden wall below a long overhang. OK, so what? And then, all is revealed: it's a huge, deeply incut ledge, like an inward-sloping pavement – about five feet deep and about fifty or sixty feet long. It's just about the very last thing you'd expect to find up here – about as incongruous as discovering a rip in the side of the Bridegroom's trousers. Come to think of it, you could accommodate his whole family in here, lying in comfortable bunks out of the wind and rain (except, being long dead and mummified, of course, they wouldn't appreciate it.)

Golly. Golly gosh! The only possible name for it comes to me immediately. I know that if ever I survive this epic, this will always and for ever be called the "Surprise Ledge". For what a fantastic surprise it is – about as welcome as being suddenly ushered into the Royal Box at the Albert Hall. Complete with a sturdy balustrade. So you can admire the grandstand view … of the Big Shitface…. And why's John so happy? Because I can see at a glance that the ledge leads straight back towards an easy-looking shallow continuation gully directly above the huge cave of "The Coffin" – which I now can see the top of, thankfully, a long way down to the right. This is a Royal Highroad indeed…. We nearly shake hands in the heat of the moment, in the manner of Tilman and Odell on Nanda Devi.

I sit down, and for a moment or two neither of us says anything. Then I find my voice and suggest that, to save time with changing over the belays, I lead along the ledge because, it being horizontal, it won't make the slightest difference in terms of safety.

And it turns out to be exactly what it looks like – nothing more than an awkward, crouching limp along a narrow furrow under the line of overhangs, made all the easier by the lip on the right, which I use as a kind of handrail to help take the weight off my knee. Then there's some snow in the furrow, which makes it a little bit more awkward, but it only seems like a matter of seconds before I've reached the welcoming confines of the gully.

Er … which is full of loose rubble. Not so good. I go up it a short way, crawling over the debris – just twenty feet or so –

When, Lo! (as Whymper would have said), I notice that the right-hand retaining wall of the gully is crested by a very enticing rib of spiky-looking rock. I drop a sling round a convenient flake on the gully wall, and then make my way very carefully up an easy series of ledges that lead out right to the crest, crawling like an invalid. But the rock is very good now: very blocky and spiky, strangely reminiscent of one of the easy buttresses on the East Face of Tryfan in North Wales. Gosh, it almost feels like home from home. Whatever next?

The Troll Wall and …

... the upper part of the Fiva Route. U=Upper Snowfield, C=Coffin, S=Surprise Ledge

And now I make yet another welcome discovery: right on the crest of this little ridge there's a large pulpit-like ledge topped by a huge, solid conical spike, offering the most perfect belay you could imagine, in an absolutely stupendous position. It's almost got a label on it saying: "Sit Here!" Above, the spiky rib continues a long way, it seems, at quite a friendly angle, but below there's nothing. Nothing but an abyss. I can't see anything until the top of the ridge we thought we should have climbed up yesterday – the one that was so obvious I said there should be a dotted line running up it. (It looks even more obvious from here.) And beyond that? … Nothing. Nothing but Romsdal – that's all! – laid out now like a rather small-scale map about five thousand feet below. There are still a few wisps of cloud drifting about down there, but I'm pleasantly surprised to see that there are also some large sun patches. It really is the most sensationally positioned belay I've ever come across: if any such stance was ever worthy of the term "The Crow's Nest", this is it. My uplifted spirits have put me in a naming mood.

I slip my biggest nylon tape sling around the spike, make myself comfortable in the pulpit, and then call out very loudly and enthusiastically: "I'm there!"

When John reaches me, in a matter of minutes, I ask him what the time is. He's obviously already looked, because he answers immediately:

"About twenty-five to one."

"Gosh," is all I can say. Because time has long since ceased to have any meaning for me.

My head drops, as I am suddenly overcome with fatigue. We haven't had any sleep now for something like thirty-six hours – and only a total of about three hours' sleep in seventy-two. But in a way it doesn't matter, because the truth is that I'm happier than I've felt in ages. There is suddenly a real chance that we might be able to get up this hideous thing, this monstrous climb. We're really starting to see the light … the light at the end of the tunnel. Surely?

12.40 pm

John has set straight off up the friendly-looking rib; and it's immediately apparent that, compared with what we've just climbed, it's a veritable stairway of good holds. We obviously still have a long way to go, but the unexpectedly straightforward nature of the climbing bodes well.

The rib leads up towards a steep, sombre headwall, like the battlements of a well-fortified castle; but it's so foreshortened that it's impossible to tell just how far away it is. Very high above me, jutting jaggedly against the sky, I can see a gigantic amorphous gargoyle, which could just conceivably be the "Owl", the very distinctive pinnacle that can be seen for miles around, which presides over the col of Ugla ("Owl") Skar, the finish of our route. If it is the Owl, then the Skar is tucked out of sight to the right somewhere.

But I'm very mindful of something I once heard someone saying in a pub in North Wales about looking for a rock feature called "the horned crag" – that when you get up there you find yourself surrounded by so many crags sprouting vague horns that trying to locate the real one is a bit like looking for "faces in a fire". So it's a good idea not to get too hopeful yet; that may not be the Owl at all, and it might not even be the summit ridge that I'm looking at.

The rope moves out steadily through my hands as John picks his way upwards; and I realize that I'm feeling more comfortable sitting in this spectacular pulpit, poised above the mighty nave of Romsdal, than I have for many a long hour. Strangely enough, my knee isn't hurting nearly so much now, after the battering it received below the "Surprise Ledge". Indeed it's become quite numb. I suppose it's Nature's way …

My eyelids droop as I gaze at the incredible panorama below me. It's much warmer up here than it was under "The Coffin", and I can hear the sound of distant water …

… *whoosh … whoosh …*

An instant later

There's a violent jolt, and I find myself staring straight into Romsdal, slumped forward, suspended over the abyss by my big pink tape sling. It's as if I'm looking down from the ceiling of a Brobdingnagian corridor at the whole of Romsdal laid out on the floor like a dark green carpet. And there's a whooshing sound like the distant roar of surf.

What? Where? Just what *am* I doing here, hanging above this giant map of Romsdal-for-real? Over a drop that *roars*, for heaven's sake. Why's it roaring?

You're on a rock climb, Gordon. Tied to the side of Store Trolltind. That roar is the roar of a thousand distant streams, distorted and amplified by these mile-high walls. Just in case you've forgotten just how big a drop it is.

There are some sharp tugs on the wet ropes, wrenching through my open hands and around my waist. *Christ, Gordon!* What are you doing? *You're not even belaying properly!* You let yourself fall asleep!

As if hearing my thoughts, John's voice, uncannily close, shouts down: "Just watch the rope, Gordon! You're snagging it!" Quite cross. "There's a lot of loose rock up here, and I don't want the rope getting caught on anything … ing."

There's still a slight echo, but the acoustic has changed completely. Although he's a long way above me, he sounds only about twenty feet away.

"You must concentrate, Gordon!"

Obviously he has no idea that the reason I "snagged" the rope was that I fell asleep.

I look up, and can just make out John's blue anorak far above me in a dark recess, but I really can't see what he's doing; and frankly, it's very difficult for me to do anything about the way the rope may or may not snag on anything. On top of which, it's a hell of a strain looking up so steeply; it gives me a crick in the back of the neck. And, anyhow, I'm just too tired, damn it. My job now is merely to pay out the ropes as smoothly as I can.

I'm gazing at the panoramic valley floor again, and suddenly I spot the minute little orange speck of our tent on a patch of grass beside a big meander of the Rauma River. It's almost too small to see with the naked eye, yet it's absolutely unmistakable. Our little home that was, that we have so foolishly deserted. Our little Cape Kennedy, our launch pad. But we're now so high above it, we could almost be going into orbit; and we may not see it again.

"OK," John calls, very close in my ears. "I'm belaying here because it looks a bit looser ahead." Well, at least that pitch has gone OK, is all I can say. I'm so tired.

And now I'm suddenly aware that I'm also ravenously hungry, probably hungrier than I've ever been in my life. My stomach is like the proverbial bottomless pit, deeper even than the trench of Romsdal below.

I can hear the chink of John's karabiners, amplified to loud metallic clonks as he rigs the belay.

"Taking in!" comes the call, almost as if he's standing next to me, shouting in my ear.

The rope comes tight on my waist.

"That's me!"

"Climb when you're ready!" comes the twinly voice, echoing off the rock walls and bouncing in my head.

"Climbing." Always climbing – as I have been so many times over the past hours, and days. And years.

"OK!" says the most familiar voice in all the world. Giving the oh-so-familiar summons. And I step onto the spike above the pulpit.

Five thousand feet above the Rauma River, in a crazy dream.

Later

On another pitch, another stance, another belay, another seat.

I'm gazing bleary-eyed across at the huge near-vertical triangular summit wall of Store Trolltind infused now with yellow light in the weak afternoon sun. My goodness, that looks good gneiss – nice climbing rock. Something for future generations, perhaps?

(Not that anyone would ever bother to come five thousand feet up here to climb it. It's just so inaccessible.) And, my goodness! – that slanting groove line looks amazing. It looks pretty holdless, but it's just possible that it's got a thin crack at the back of it, and you could layback up it all the way. Wowee! What standard would that be, I wonder? … Probably at least 6A. Hard Extreme, certainly … You'd probably have to take a hanging belay in that little alcove above the overhangs. Just imagine what that would be like. Absolutely amazing.

Mind you, I wonder just what we would look like from up there? I imagine it looks pretty impressive. Two minute little insects, one blue, the other orange, connected by two fine strands of yellow and red nylon, making their way almost imperceptibly up this huge rock amphitheatre, this great gash in the face of Herr Troll.

And it probably also looks pretty amazing from out on that huge shoulder of Nordre Trolltind. Of course there's no one up there. I'm sure I'd be able to see people if there were. There's no sign of life anywhere; it's all completely deserted. Come to think of it, I wonder just how often anyone stands on the top of any of these silent summits?

There's a very loud crack, somewhere very far away, like a miniature explosion – like the biggest banger you can buy – followed by a horrible splitting sound.

I glance back at the very face I've just been looking at – tracing my "rock routes of the future" – and very far up, not far below the summit, I see a puff of smoke. Then a little cluster of pebbles detaching themselves and starting to fall down the face in slow motion. I realize immediately, as I watch in mesmerised horror, that the largest one – shaped like a tombstone – must be at least the size of a caravan.

Jesus bloody wept!

It hits a ledge opposite me, and there is a second sensational explosion as it breaks into several smaller pieces, each about the size of an Austin Mini. Then they glance off some slabs, break into dozens more fragments, and plunge out of sight down the main gully in a huge volley of explosions, echoed and magnified by the vast retaining walls, fading away until there's complete silence once again.

"Bloody hell," says John, about sixty feet above me. "Did you see that?"

Did I see that?

"Of course I did!"

The words have scarcely left my lips when there's a stupendous din from the depths as the whole fusillade finally begins to hit the ravenous pit of the screes, lying in wait some five thousand feet below. It goes on for quite a while, before fading to a menacing silence.

A strong smell of cordite wafts up on the cool updraft, pungent with malevolence.

"A good thing we're not still in the gully!" John says, verbalizing the very obvious.

"And a *bit!*" I call up, imitating Gary in our local climbing club.

John turns back to the climb, and carries on where he left off. As if nothing's changed. But he's scarcely gone another twenty feet before there's another resounding crack, and yet more debris cascades in a waterful of rock and dust down the face. *Holy Moly!* The Trolltind world, it is exploding, violence flaring, boulders plunging; and the whole terrifying sequence of events is repeated, this time on an even greater scale.

The rope is stationary. John has stopped to watch again – this horror show of fireworks without fire, accompanied by that pungent smell. A dismal scene that Dante would have relished.

And once again there's a resounding multiple echo as the whole lot eventually crashes onto the screes.

Well, Tony Willmott did say it was "a cracking route", didn't he? I smile ironically.

The old petrified gnome of the Owl, who knows all about these things, having witnessed them countless times before, is still gazing into space, absolutely impassive. Completely unmoved.

(… *Thank goodness! … I wouldn't want that lot on top of me!*)

John starts to climb again.

Some time, much later

I awake with a start, having fallen asleep on my slings again. I haven't admitted to John that I've been falling asleep, but he's probably guessed it. All afternoon, he's been doing a brilliant job with the route-finding, the belays, all the rope work – everything. I've lost track of the number of pitches we must have climbed since The Crow's Nest. We're in slow motion. At least, I am. I can't see John's watch, so I can't confirm that anything's progressing at all. That anything's changing. There's nothing to suggest it.

Except that the rib has now faded out into an indefinite area of loose, rubbly ledges below a steep and intimidating wall, presenting a formidable barrier below the skyline, so foreshortened that it's of indeterminate height. John's scouting around beneath it, looking for the best way, trying to find a weakness. Once again, it seems, it's the old, old question: just where in the hell does the route go? He's taking extreme care on all the loose rock, poised directly above me, moving about up there without a sound, like a cat. Testing everything very carefully, as if he's climbing up a precarious pile of large ostrich eggs. No, I don't think there are any ostriches up here, but there are certainly a couple of young and inexperienced idiots who've been acting like ostriches – watched over all the time by the so-called "wise old" Owl.

Actually John is making sounds now, he's muttering to himself – his voice amplified, as if only a few feet away – complaining about the rock being very shattered, the route not being obvious, and no sign that anyone's ever been here. He's having a right old grumble. "Below!"

A massive missile, full of malice, whacks onto the side of the wall above me and goes whining past into the depths. Emphasising our precariousness, and filling the air with question marks of lingering cordite.

It's a headwall, yes, but is it *the* headwall? Or is there another one beyond it? How far, really, are we from the col of Ugla Skar? The view is so restricted that it's impossible to tell, but I suspect it's still hundreds of feet, judging by the height of the Big Troll opposite us.

All these questions with no answers. This being a mountain without answers, a problem without a solution, a riddle wrapped in mist, a climb without an end. And always that ringing, which goes on and on and on: Ping, ping, ping; ping, *ping, ping* – that endless musical scale, accompanied by the drumroll of rock falls, large and small – incessantly. Even the large ones have just become part of the routine. Always the same story, climbing for ever, while the rocks boom, the stones whizz past, and John's karabiners tinkle like bells. The bells of the Trolls.

"God, this is a dangerous place!" John says as he lashes me onto the mountain yet again when I reach him. He looks at me rather intensely, clearly alarmed at just how woozy I've become.

"All going down the Main Gully … " I mumble, half asleep.

"Yes. Hmm!" He gives an ironic little laugh-cum-sniff. That's all. No further comment. Then: "Are you really OK?"

"Yeah, I just fell asleep for a moment down there – that's all."

The last few pitches he's been tugging me a bit harder. Obviously trying to keep me awake, as well as help me to climb. I've been going so slowly he's obviously concerned that I'm fading. All the time his insistent tugging of the rope has been saying: You just *mustn't* stop; please, please come on; get on with it. Keep on coming. You've got to make it. We've *got* to get up this thing.

Now we've changed the guard at Trolltind's Palace, and I'm sitting beside a narrow chimney like a damp sentry box set into a dark, vertical wall. Only the belay slings are preventing me from rolling forward with fatigue, on this climb without end. I almost can't remember life when I wasn't climbing this route. When I was not forever stuck in this grueling, granitic, knee-grinding routine. Grovelling at the feet of the Troll and all his ugly, spiky kin, including his ridiculous pet Owl. Yes, I am become a "Troll-child", curled up now with bent knees in a foetal position, resigned to my Troll fate … holding a wet rope that goes up for ever, ever so slowly through my hands, and then stops completely, because time itself has stopped.

A strangely distant voice, almost cheeky in the way it interrupts my thoughts, rings out:

"I'm there! – I'm at the top!" Triumphant as a distant hunting horn or trumpet.

What? *WHAT!*

Did I hear him right? *Surely it's impossible!*

But I realize that the acoustic of his voice is so very different, so far away now, that he really must be out in the open. But perhaps it's not the top, but some subsidiary thing?

"Are you sure?" I shout, my voice quaking, croaking.

"Yes! – I'm standing on the top!"

"Can you see the other side of the ridge?"

"Yes, miles – miles and miles!"

"You're on the ridge?"

"*Yes!* – I'm on the horizontal!"

Have I ever been so happy?

It's all so sudden, all so totally unexpected. An impossible dream come true. Then, "Taking in!" – and real time resumes and the rope rushes upwards with a new vigour, as if raised from the dead.

"That's me!" I'm fighting back the tears of relief and joy … "Climbing!" I choke, and I start up the final chimney.

About ten minutes later

I'm in a deep, dirty slot, deep in the heart of the mountain – so deep that Romsdal is just a rectangular museum piece seen through the slit of a vertical letter box. It's base, the valley floor, seeming impossibly far beneath me.

Don't rush. Patience! All our troubles are now over – we've just got an easy three-hour walk down to Stegfoss to do, and it would be stupid to screw things up by further damaging my knee in this final chimney. Try to do this last bit as well as possible. Try to arrive at the top in good shape. *In good shape?* Ha! At least you've still got your sense of humour, Gordon!

John has the ropes as tight as ships' hawsers, as I scrabble and struggle, trying to be careful of my knee. That's a lot easier said than done in a chimney, when you have to use the knees to make upward progress; and its throbbing dome is getting scrunched excruciatingly the whole time on the opposite wall. But it doesn't matter, it really doesn't matter. We've done it, we've done it! I'm crying with tears of mere pain; and the greatest joy I've ever felt.

A light appears, a bright hole of sky. *"The Hole"!* Yes, the Hole – with the ropes going up through it, tight as rods. At last the secret of the hole is revealed. It's just a gap behind a big chockstone blocking the very top of the chimney. At the very top of the route – just when it's all over! Rather like a difficult crux pitch on a rock climb I know where the guidebook talks about a good finishing hold, but actually you can't reach it until you're past all the difficulties, and it's no longer of the slightest use.

"Escape by a hole and chimney to Ugla Skar"! Well, the guidebook couldn't even get that right: it's a "chimney and hole", that way round – with the hole right at the very top, when it's all over.

There are some great moments in life, and this is one of them. In spirit I come out of the hole like a cork out of a champagne bottle, but in reality I roll over the rim like a sack of potatoes. From the vertical to the horizontal. From dark to light. I don't even attempt to stand up; I swivel round on the rough gravelly top.

Vast spaces; mountains as far as the eye can see; distant fjords. Too much, really, to take in, and too bright after the black confines of the chimney. Cloud above, but clear straight ahead to the west.

John is sitting some distance away on a low boulder, with his back to the view and his legs out in front of him. Looking utterly exhausted, as shattered as the mountain itself.

I mutter something about "I can't believe it, I really can't believe it," and then, quietly: "What's the time?"

"4.30,"

he says, and *"PM!",* he adds with a chuckle, just in case I've got confused. Which I have, really – having being incarcerated for so long on this timeless Troll fortress of grotesque granitic gargoyles that has nothing whatever to do with human life, or any standard scales of measurement.

I spot a sloping rock shelf on the other side of the col, complete with a low wall that will act as a suitable backrest, because the first thing I need to do is sit somewhere comfortable and take stock of my knee. As John lets go of my ropes, and I stumble thirty feet or so across the rubbly col to reach it, I have to confess that I'm feeling rather proud. Almost heroic, dare I say it? That we've not only managed to extricate ourselves from a near-death experience, but we've even managed to do the route. It's what you call a rather "big tick", given the circumstances. Never before in my climbing career have I felt quite such a sense of achievement.

Directly behind the "seat", I can see a friendly-looking, blocky ridge leading directly up to the summit of Store Trolltind. It's temptingly close, just a few hundred feet it seems, but neither of us mentions it, because it is of absolutely no consequence now and climbing any further is out of the question. All that matters is that we've done our route, and reached safety. Now we must get down.

I take off my sack and sit on the rock shelf, completely relaxed for the first time in two days. I undo my waist knot, which is very tight from all the resting that I've been doing on the rope, and then take a huge swig of water. I'm elated, really. All our worries are over. We just have an easy three to four-hour descent to Stegfoss according to the guidebook – Tony Charlton told us it's just "an easy downhill walk with no technical difficulties at all".

Hopefully we'll be able to find a nice stream soon, and get some fresh water, because this stuff, absolutely full of grit, is really horrible.

John has gathered the rope in a great damp pile, and is now stuffing it back into his sack. "I won't bother to coil it yet," he says, "since we won't be needing it any more. I'll wait till we get to Stegfoss." I don't blame him, because apart from anything else, coiling a three-hundred-foot rope is really quite tiring, and we're just too exhausted now. I must say I'm quite glad to see the back of it, though.

John also has a big drink of water, and then brings his rucksack over and joins me on the rock ledge, while I turn my attention to my knee, which I'm really rather dreading.

I pull back my breeches and find it's in an even worse state than I was expecting. The bandage I made last night is hanging in tatters, and has fallen right down, all loose, so that the great big purple and yellow globe of my ex-knee – about five inches in diameter – is now exposed to view. So I'm going to have to completely re-bandage it.

John has problems of his own. "Just look at my hands!" They're all white and leprous in appearance – all wrinkled and full of little cuts.

"But … where're your mitts?"

"They fell apart! Wore right through, so I dumped them. Chain stitching completely went. Fell apart with all the hauling."

I haven't been using my Millar mitts either, because they became unpleasantly wet and soggy, but my hands aren't in nearly such a bad way as John's. But there's an orange stain from the rope.

I cut away all the old adhesive bandage round my knee with the little scissors, place a new pad of cotton wool on it, and then carefully get to work with the re–bandaging.

"How's it feeling?"

"Pretty bad, but no worse really. It's sort of gone numb. I'm just going to have to go very slowly on the descent."

"Let's look at the map and the guidebook," John says, as I carefully wind the bandage round my knee in a figure of eight. "They're in the top of your sack, aren't they?"

John reads from book. "Three hours, Grade One, from *the top of Store Trolltind*; so I suppose about two-and-half hours down to Stegfoss from here."

"But it's probably going to take us at least four, maybe five, with my knee. So it could be as late as ten-thirty before we get to Stegfoss. We should be able to get some food there."

John's looking at the map … "Where's Stegfoss? I don't see it on the map."

"I couldn't see it either. What does the guidebook say?"

"Well, it's in Isterdal, at the start of the 'Ordinary Route'. It just says: 'From the viewing place above the waterfalls at Stegfoss, follow the cairned path up into the hanging valley' – that's obviously the hanging valley below us, and that's Isterdal beyond." John points into the haze.

"I can't see any path down there. Can you?"

"No, but we're too far above it. I'm sure it'll be obvious further down."

I'm winding the self-adhesive bandage round my knee now, on top of the ordinary one, so that it's starting to look a little bit like the head of an Egyptian mummy.

"It's odd they don't mark the path or Stegfoss on the map. It doesn't even mark Store Trolltind, does it?"

"Well, Tony Willmott warned us the map was crap. He said it's the one they used in the War, with lots of place names removed to fool the Germans."

"Well, that's a fat lot of good!"

"Anyhow, we've got to look out for a pinnacle called Stabben … I suppose it means 'Knife' or something. That's where we go down. I'm sure it'll all make sense once we get there."

"God, I wish there was a helicopter! Or a cable car!" Now that the elation of getting to the top has worn off, I'm feeling very, very tired, and appallingly hungry. I put the first-aid kit away, and pull the loose, torn breeches over the big bandaged "football" of my knee. Then I do quite a hefty push-up with my arm to get stood up, because I've got very stiff since I've sat down.

Aaghh! God, my knee feels weak now! I hope I'm going to be able to manage this …

"You OK?" John looks a bit anxious, because he can see I'm in pain. "Actually, my legs are feeling bloody tired, too," he says – I suppose to try and cheer me up – "From all the winching, belaying. I've been bending down and then standing up again, all day, hauling you. Really tiring!"

One last thing: a summit rock. I pick a suitable loose stone as a memento and put it in my right pocket with the guidebook. It's actually more than a memento, because I'm quite superstitious and perhaps it'll bring us luck.

"So, ve go, yah?" John says, a little less cheerfully than he did yesterday morning.

About 6.00 pm

We've descended a short way from Ugla Skar, and found a faint horizontal path which has now run out in a shallow gully. Above us is a very obvious knifelike pinnacle, which we reckon must be the thing the guidebook calls "Stabben", so we've started to descend. Actually, I prefer going straight down like this because I can take a lot of my weight on my hands on either side of my bum; and when I get tired I can simply sit down.

It's going well, and we've lost a lot of height surprisingly fast. But now John, who's a long way ahead, has stopped.

"Everything OK?" I call.

"No – this doesn't feel right at all. It's getting far too steep, and it doesn't look as though anyone's been down this way."

Suddenly I have a gnawing doubt. "John, I think the book said the Ordinary Route goes past a *second* col – called Brur Skar, or something like that."

I'm looking at the back of his head.

"Oh, shit! You're right! – " His head whips round. "What a cock up! We're going to have to go all the way back up to the traverse line. There's no other choice."

When John gets to me, I can see he's really pissed off, but fortunately he's not blaming me, even though I was the one who was keen to head straight down into the hanging valley at the first opportunity.

Climbing back up is at least as bad as I feared. I have to use my arms so much to take the weight off my knee that I'm feeling absolutely knackered. And I've got very hot. More wasted calories!

I was really hoping that we weren't going to have to climb up a single foot more today, and now we're having to bloody well re-ascend about four hundred feet … And we've still got five thousand feet to descend!… We're only a few hundred feet from Ugla Skar and things are already going badly wrong. What a waste of time and energy!

Only three weeks ago, I was reading an article by Tom Patey, called "Apes and Ballerinas" in the latest issue of *Mountain* magazine, and he said – it was meant to be funny – words to the effect that "a proficient mountaineer needs to satisfy only three criteria" – I think those were his words. "He mustn't fall off. He mustn't lose the route. And he mustn't waste time."

How I chuckled! Well, now the Stainforth twins have done all three. It's really not so funny now.

A cheerful shout from John above. "I've found it!"

It takes me ten minutes to get up to him: he's standing on a neat little path, just the same as the one the other side of the gully. There's even a faint patch of very old red paint on a smooth rock step next to it. It's obviously a route marker.

"We just didn't look hard enough," John says. "We've really got to keep our wits about us, Gordon! We can't afford to make a single other mistake like that."

You don't have to tell me, John! Anyhow, it's a huge relief to be back on the proper path – it turns out to be very easy – and in a few minutes we're ascending very slightly to a big notch in the skyline ridge, which looks rather as if it's been used for target practice by the Russians, or something, and has been blasted through by a ballistic missile. Obviously this is what the guidebook refers to as "Brur Skar".

We find it's like a pavement in the sky, with a very sharp edge. We've been down in the void for thirty-six hours, fighting for our lives, and it's sickening now to look back over the edge. It's the kind of drop that hits you in the stomach.

"Gosh!" says John – and there's that "roar" again. The drop that roars at you like surf. The Troll Wall on our right plunges down plumb vertical for a mile, bristling with hideous overhangs. We lie down and poke our heads right over the edge. The wall directly beneath is literally overhanging, and the screes thousands of feet below look absolutely flat from here, as flat as the valley floor beyond it – even though we know they're really very steep. A mist wreathing around above it heightens the ominous mood. Down to the left we can see the whole of the lower half of the Fiva Route – the main snowfield and all the introductory slabs, withering away into the distance. And again I feel proud of the sheer height we've climbed, just what we've done.

"Oh gosh, John, look, there's our tent!" That unmistakable little orange speck, like a bright grain of sand on a patch of green by that huge bend in the river. It looks very lonely. And even as I watch, a thin veil of cloud drifts across and obscures it from view. Gone.

Across the valley I see something more worrying. The weather is obviously turning. A huge bank of cloud has rolled over the ridge on the far side, its base at least two thousand feet lower than we are – and it's coming our way.

I stand up again. "I don't want to see Romsdal again," I say, "until I'm actually standing in it, right back at the very bottom!"

"Yeah, let's get the hell out of here!"

We start back along the traverse. All that matters now is getting to Stegfoss and food – presuming we can get some there – and getting into our sleeping bags.

Very soon there's a tricky looking step of fifty feet.

John turns at the top of it. "Are you OK?"

"Yeah, absolutely fine," even though I'm hobbling like an Old Man. The rock's got big chunky steps, and it turns out to be an absolute doddle even with "my knee". In a moment we're passing the famous pinnacles, Trollkjerringa and Trollgrubben – the Old Troll Woman and the Old Troll Man – that are mentioned in most of the tourist brochures. Even from the back they look quite impressive jutting against the sky. The Old Woman, the taller and more impressive of the two, comes first. "Old Battle Axe" would be a better name for it, I think. The Old Man is meant to have a face on it, but the only Old Man's Face I can see around here, right now, is John's. Up beyond it, there's cloud starting to wisp around the summit of Trollryggen.

The cloud has also come right down on the mountain we can see straight ahead of us, with big snowfields running across it. But not to worry – our route doesn't go over there. We're on a very easy path now – who could imagine it would be quite this easy? – and, for extra reassurance, every so often, we pass another faint red disk of old weathered paint on the rock as a route marker. Our whole nightmare really is over. It's just a matter now of following the markers.

Some time later, perhaps an hour

We've been carefully following the path, painstakingly ensuring that we're following the red markers as the ground has become easier and the path less distinct. It hasn't been too bad for me because traversing a slope like this suits my bent left leg, and I can

take a lot of my weight on my left hand.

But now we've found ourselves standing beside a huge scree slope just below the cloud level. Neither of us can make out any trace of a path going across it – it's just vanished completely – there's not a marker in sight. Obviously we must now be below Stabben, so this is where we descend into the hanging valley. Though it's a bit odd there aren't any markers of any kind.

So we decide to simply head straight down the scree towards a tarn of vivid turquoise-green glacier water.

I've been on far steeper scree slopes, of course, but never with a badly injured knee. It's quite unstable and very coarse, consisting of rough fragments that vary between about six inches and a foot across; the only way I can manage it is by sitting on my bum and taking most of the weight on my hands. Even so, my injured leg gets badly jarred with every downward move, as I bounce my right foot down, in effect descending in little jerks. I'm trying to go as fast as possible but it's desperately slow work and John soon leaves me far behind … But at least it's getting us very directly down to the tarns mentioned in the guide.

I can see John waiting for me about a hundred feet below, being very careful not to lose sight of me. I'm still a bit baffled why there aren't any cairns or markers of any kind.

Later still

This really is one of the loneliest, most desolate landscapes I've ever seen, consisting only of wet rock, scree, and snow patches. Nothing else. It's like a great black-walled hall with a grey cloud ceiling, that's completely cut off from the world.

All the way down, John's been picking the best line, and then having to wait for me for about ten minutes, every ten minutes. We're on much finer scree now, which is really easy for him, but truly vile for me because I'm having to use my hands the whole way, and the rock is really sharp-edged. They've been getting cut to shreds, so I've now put on my thick woollen Dachstein mitts for protection.

My arms are now so tired I'm not sure quite how much longer I'm going to be able to do this. Yes, it's real Hemingway stuff again: now it's *A Farewell to Arms!* I give an ironic smile, shot with pain. And, because my right knee is having to do most of the work, it's now hurting almost as much as the left. I don't want A Farewell to Knees as well, or worse, A Farewell to Legs …

My Dachsteins are getting completely ruined, of course, but it doesn't matter. Nothing matters now except getting off this horrible mountain.

John's waiting for me at the bottom of the scree, where the angle eases right off (but, sadly, beyond him it looks a lot more bouldery again).

"I'm sorry, John, but I really can't go any faster."

"I know, don't worry. All that matters is that we just keep going. We'll get there!"

"Any sign of the path?"

"No." John's looking very cheesed off, and somewhat puzzled. But he clearly doesn't want to share his worries, because he knows that I've got enough on my plate at the moment. So he heads off again, picking his way through the boulders.

Even now that we're nearly on the horizontal, I'm still only able to go at about one fifth of John's speed. So, once again, every hundred yards or so he's having to wait about five or ten minutes for me to catch him up. All the time he is recceing the easiest possible line ahead.

I am become a quasi-human beetle, crawling round and over boulders, up and down. There are even some small "climbing" moves. It's desperate. I seem to be going slower and slower. We weren't counting on this at all. I'm sure the guidebook implied there was a path the whole way – didn't it? I'll have another look at it when I reach John.

He's looking at the map again. I suppose it's something to do to fill in the time while he's waiting for me. "Well, we're passing the tarns now," he says. "At least the first one. There's only one marked on the map, which is a bit odd. Storgrovbotnen."

"Whatever that means."

"Well, 'botnen' probably means bottom, and 'stor's' big. So, 'Big Grove Bottom'?"

"Or Big Grave?" Then wish I hadn't said it. Because we are very seriously famished now, and we're not going to be able to go on for many more hours like this without any sustenance. We're weakening all the time. It's very serious because it means the clock is ticking, and there will come a time when our energy will give out completely. I think I must be "living off my own body" now, as they say. We've just got to get to Stegfoss.

John's peering into the distance, at the far end of the lake, which is fringed by snow and boulders.

"Hang on! That's a hut, isn't it?" Peering intently.

"Ah, yes! So it is. Good heavens!" By the shore at the end, nestling among some large boulders, I can see a very neat little hut with a pointed roof. "Obviously some kind of boat hut. I suppose."

This is the best discovery that we've made for ages. Signs of humanity at last! Even better, there's bound to be a path leading up to it. I say that to him. "It would seem logical, wouldn't it?"

Would it? Since when has logic had anything to do with the Trolltindane?

I start to hum as we make our way towards it.

"And the path was deep and wide from footsteps leading to our cabin …"

It seems appropriate enough. I'm so tired I can only hum it very quietly, in a very fragmented, breathless kind of way: the disjointed mumbling of a disjointed invalid:

"… And late at night … a hand would knock … and there would stand a stranger –"

"Hell's bells!" says John – he's stopped. "… And buckets of blood!" He's fuming.

The hut is not a hut at all. It's just another boulder with a pointed top.

"Shucks," I say quietly. Can things get worse? Probably. And up behind the boulders the most repulsive, inhuman slabs of wet rock disappear up into the cloud … Oh, please God, get me down, get me out of here …

Just beyond the "hut" boulder we come to a stream that issues from the end of the tarn. At least this is a chance to fill up with fresh water, because we haven't had any for hours, and my throat is quite sore. Unfortunately it's still full of granite dust, and icy cold. God knows what it's doing to my stomach – I've already been getting stomach cramps for quite a while. We just sip it, drinking as little as possible.

"That's why the water's that milky green colour," John says. "It's all the rock dust in it."

It's also a chance for me to wash my hands, which got really filthy before I put my Dachsteins on. The little cracks all round my finger nails are worse than ever, and quite sore. I think they're going slightly septic from the orange dye that's come out of the rope. So at last this is a chance to wash that off. My lips are quite sore, too, and cracked. So I rinse them too.

John's looking at the map again. Not that there's very much to study, since there's nothing on it around Storgrovbotnen except a few contour lines.

Suddenly he looks up very positively and cheerfully. "Gosh, I hadn't thought of that before! The river's called the "Storgrova". So I think "Steg" could be a contraction – or whatever – of Storgrova. 'Foss' means waterfall. So Stegfoss is Storgrova Waterfall!"

It's a pretty convincing argument. "Good thinking! I'm surprised we didn't think of it earlier. But where on earth's the bloody path? … And the other tarns? I don't see any."

"Well, there could be more, lower down, hidden out of sight. And this is the hanging valley, alright, because we can see the end of it now, or at least a subsidiary lip. It looks much grassier down there, so we should be able to find the path easily enough."

"What's that?" I say.

"What?"

We listen.

"A peg hammer. I keep on hearing it."

"I can't …"

"I think I've heard it several times in the last half hour. I keep on thinking I can hear a peg hammer."

"I think you're imagining it."

No, I can definitely hear it. Echoing round the crags … and in my head. Yet sounding very far away. Far and near.

Ping, ping, ping, ping, ping …

"Anyhow, what on earth's the time?"

"Twenty to ten. We must get moving again."

Much later (I daren't ask John the time now)

At last we've left most of the boulders and scree behind, and have come out onto a steep slope of nice grassy, heathery stuff. John's looking very, very tired, since he's been doing all the detailed route-finding, weaving through the boulders, always looking for the easiest route, often trying several alternative ways. I'm sure the going is going to get a lot easier now. "The going?" Going. It's going on for ever. For ever and ever. On and on. I hope it's not "going, going, gone". Because my hunger is really eating at me now, and I'm feeling rather feverish. My face is all flushed, hot, and glowing. I can tell I'm living off my body now. Starving, in other words. My body is literally gnawing at itself for food. Burning itself out. Fiva fever.

Just where is this *bloody path*? This famous, non-existent, fanciful path? Just where in the hell is it? In this hell. With it's anvil chorus of continual hammering. *Ping, ping, ping, ping, ping …*

John's got this ludicrous theory now that "Maybe there isn't a proper path, and people just pick their own way?"

I lean back against the comfortable heathery slope and simply sink into it, completely exhausted. It really is very comfortable.

A voice is singing now.

Why, why, why, why, why?…

… I wonder …

Why?

– Wailing away.

"Gordon, wake up!" John's prodding me. "We mustn't fall asleep. We've got to get down!"

Oh God, try to levitate.

"Christ! Did you hear that?" John says.

"No, what?"

"I just heard some shouts. I definitely heard voices."

I listen and listen, but I can't hear a thing – except water, water … everywhere. And then … Oh, yes … *So there is!*… There's a kind of burble, as if several people are arguing about something, or laughing even …

It's very loud now … In fact, it's a real hubbub this evening, with everyone shouting to be heard. And *telling stories*.

"The top pitch of *Bovine* is amazing – if you don't linger! Fantastic jugs."

"Isn't it a bit scary?" John's voice.

"Yeah – but it's *so easy!* You know it's seventy feet overhanging, and you just go!"

Another voice: "But that first corner! *Shit man!* It's diabolically hard. You've got to do this really beefy swing out left at the top. I thought it was 5B."

Another voice: "We did *Canopy* last week – you don't want to go there! There were jugs on the first pitch that still had blood in them. Still warm, it was!"

His mate: "… *And brains!*… "

"No, I shouldn't go there for a bit!"

John: "Yes, I've always heard it's the biggest chopper in Wales!"

And now he's calling to me:

"*Gordon!*…

"Gordon! – Wake up! We've just got to keep moving."

"What?" I open my eyes. Oh, shit! "Oh, sorry, John, I just nodded off again."

I'm lying sprawled back in the heather. It's very comfortable. But, God, I'm feeling hungry! I've got to eat something. I suppose

I could always try eating some of these plants.

My knowledge of flora is rudimentary, to put it mildly – I can just about tell a dandelion from a buttercup. And now I really haven't a clue what might work as food. I've often chewed rose petals in our garden at home, and now I can see a little plant beside me with bright green pointed leaves that look as if they might just be nutritious.

I take off my soggy Dachsteins. They're filthy and ragged. All the wool's been pulled. Pretty much wrecked, really; but it doesn't matter. Nothing matters, except getting off this mountain.

I snap off one of the leaves, and bite off the end. It's all rough on the underside. And I chew it. It's really bitter – *Aaagh!*… Ugh! I spit it out.

Now I rip out a rather peculiar piece of heather with some even more peculiar little berries on it. Perhaps they'll work? I try chewing one. It's really hard, almost like wood, and very bitter.

John's looking at me in astonishment. "What on earth are you eating?"

I'm chewing hard, trying desperately to break it down. I spit it out in disgust.

"Heather."

"What!"

"Well, I thought with a bit of luck something round here might just be edible. You never know."

"Anyhow, that's not heather."

"Well, saxifrage, then!… I wonder if this'll work?"

I stick another sample of a strange dark green leafy plant in my mouth. I chew like a rabbit.

"God, you mustn't do that, Gordon! It's bloody silly. It might be poisonous."

It's very sour. I spit it out immediately.

"But it could make such a difference," I say, "if we could only find something that works and gives us a few calories."

John's sat down. His eyelids are drooping.

"Well, I'm not doing it …"

And now I get bold. How about some of that rather succulent looking dark red moss? I take a bunch of it in my thumb and fingers and stick a little bit in my mouth. It's very gritty, and more or less tasteless. Maybe there's some goodness in it if I chew it for long enough?

But no such luck here, either. It's equally revolting, and absolutely devoid of nutrition. But I'm not going to give up that easily. There must be something that works. I try leaves of all shades of green, bushy grey-blue moss, coarse grass – even roots. Nothing works. It's all either stringy, or earthy, or woody – and all completely inedible.

"Euggh!… Eunoch! Arnich! Cnicht! Sgurr Jerrak! Uick! Eich! Liathach!"

Suddenly I have become fluent in Gaelic; a truly peckish Pict.

This is probably how cave men used to speak – the inhabitants of the Trolltindane – up here, hundreds of thousands of years ago. How they still do. The moss-eaters of Stor Grove Bottom.

It's hopeless. I could probably eat a worm now, if I could find one.

"This is a real bummer," I say out loud.

John doesn't even bother to answer. I glance at him. He's leaning back in the heather, fast asleep.

All this little piece of obscure flower- and herb-tasting has done has left me with an even more horrible taste in my mouth than there was before.

I get out my water-bottle, take a swig, gargle, and spit it out.

I lie back again. Surely there's no harm in resting – just for a moment? It's just so comfortable.

Some time

"Gordon, sorry to trouble you, but I've just 'ad Mister Bleeding 'Olt on the phone again about those anvils. He says Bedford Components 'ave been onto 'im again, and they're getting really narked. You've got to try and get Arthur to take off the 551C cams, and get back to the anvils."

"I keep on trying, Betty! I tried again before lunch, but he just wouldn't listen to me. He just said 'Sod off!'"

"Well, I tell you, Mr 'Olt's really on his 'igh 'orse now! I 'aven't 'eard 'im so flaming uppity since we lost the ratchets order. He says the anvils are now absolutely top priority. You've got to go back to Arthur and 'ave another go. Just say Betty says so. That'll get 'im! Just tell 'im Betty says to stop dilly-dallying and take 'em off!"

"OK." Oh, crikey. So, now I'm making my way back through the clangorous din of the Press Shop, with all that ceaseless, pile-driving hammering and thumping; and go through into the Capstan Shop. The foreground whine is fantastic, and in the background there are those hammers going endlessly … Pong, pong, pong, pong, *pong!* It's like a dungeon in hell.

Old Arthur, the Shop Steward, is bent over his big gold lathe in his blue overalls like a wizard up to no good.

"Arthur?"

He pretends not to notice me above the shrill whine and the thumping and banging. He always pretends to be deaf. He's wrinkling up his nose as he watches the little strip of metal peeling off under the router. Then he looks up. He's got a very ugly face, all pocked and pitted. It's a most peculiar complexion, scarcely human, all leathery like an old Alpine guide, only with black oil smears on it and, worse, a nasty, uncooperative frown. The cacophony is deafening, and there's milky swarf gushing out of the bottom of the lathe and going all over my nice new leather shoes. So I'm standing in a puddle of milk. The hammering sound is relentless. *Ping, ping, ping* … Pung, pung, pung, pung, *ping!* I lean sideways and put my hand on the greasy railing.

And feel wet grass.

Oh my God, oh my God, where am I?

I'm back here, right in the middle of nowhere, surrounded by wet heather and rock. Dank, dark, grey, soulless, lifeless. The bottom of the cloud is wafting across the thousand-foot-high ruined rock fortress opposite me. Great furrows of grey-brown rotten rock tower up into the murk, with multiple ribs and ridges, separated by enormous grooves. As if it was once rasped at several millennia ago by gigantic claws, and then left for dead.

God, I hate this desolate ruin of a landscape, this most alien, most barren, most hellishly bleak place. Perhaps I'm not really here? … *Sorry!* This is your new home, you moss-eating fool!

Has any living thing ever been here before? Before *us?* There's not the slightest sign, the slightest hint, of life anywhere to be seen. Just me, and John … and Mister Bleeding 'Olt.

God I hate this mountaineering lark.

Dead silence. Save for the faint giggling of a million streams and waterfalls. And John snoring faintly in the heather beside me.

I thump him. We must move – we *must* keep moving. If we fall asleep now in our damp clothes, out on this open mountainside, we might never wake up, and just stay up here for ever, having died of exposure.

John grunts something, mumbles, and we stumble slowly to our feet, very stiff, cold, and damp. My right leg is aching painfully, and my bent left leg is locked solid and completely numb. I'm shivering a bit, so I start to rub my right leg and hop up and down on it to try and get the circulation going; and then I start to lumber down the heathery hillside like a reeling Action Man on a flat battery. Forcing myself to try and go a bit faster. Anything to warm up. Hopping on my right leg.

So we go on – down and down the gentle slope – slumping back every ten minutes or so into the heather when our legs give way. Shouting at each other to keep ourselves awake, not to fall asleep, to keep going. Keep going! With all the time that ringing going on and on in my head: *Ping, ping, ping – Ding, ding, ding –* Dong, dong, dong!

I've got to sit down again.

Dreamtime …

That smile! God, she's going to kill me with that Norwegian smile. Just how can anyone have teeth as perfect as that? I guess it's all the fish they eat, or something. And those chilling blue eyes, they're going right through me … It's quite obvious that the only reason she was put on this planet was to have sex …

"Gordon!

"Gordon!

"Wake up!"

God knows when

"Look!"

Who? What? *Where's she gone?*

"What?"

"Look over there. Can you see what I can see?"

What? … Where?

Oh my God! My heart leaps.

I just can't believe it! It's really the very last thing on earth I was expecting to see. The best thing I could possibly imagine.

There are a couple of people on the crest of the hanging valley. And they're coming straight towards us. Clear as Norwegian daylight at midnight. Large as life.

Good grief. Our troubles really are over now. I feel like crying with joy, but I'm just too tired. "Good heavens," I say. And I really mean it. This is the kind of thing that really makes one believe in prayer. Just one of those incredible things in life that happens just when you're least expecting it. It really is almost too good to be true. *Thank God.* And just when things were looking so bad.

John says: "They've just appeared. They definitely weren't there a minute ago. They just suddenly appeared there." I haven't seen him looking so happy for yonks. "Are they really coming this way?" I wonder. "Looks like it."

I still almost can't believe my eyes. But it's true. I'd just about ruled out the possibility of ever seeing anyone up here. I don't know why; it's silly, but I just had. It's pretty illogical. Why shouldn't anyone walk up here? But –

"I wonder what on earth they're doing – coming up here at this time of night? – Whatever it is now."

"It's twenty to eleven. It's very late … I think they might have come to look for *us*."

"Who?"

"Well, it could be Hugh and Brian, couldn't it?"

"Ah – that's a thought."

"They could have got to Fiva Farm and seen our notice on the tent and guessed we've had some kind of epic. And they're coming up the descent route in the hope of finding us."

My God, I'm grateful. "Bloody good of them," I say.

It's really quite moving – to think that some people – perhaps even Hugh and Brian – have come right up here at this very late hour to look for us. I'm absolutely elated, and not a little moved. The sense of camaraderie is palpable.

"Good God!" John exclaims. "I'm sure it's Hugh and Brian! The stocky one on the left – that's the way Hugh walks. That's his walk!"

I'll have to confess it does look very like him, the way he's walking. Dear old Hugh! I must say he is a brick, he really is. An absolute brick. A real rock. Tears of emotion are welling up. I have an overwhelming sense of gratitude.

"And, of course, the other really good thing", I say, "is that because they've come up the descent route, they'll know the path exactly. So there won't be the slightest chance of getting lost now."

"Yeah, they must have come up from the viewing place by the waterfall."

Suddenly we're very wide awake, our senses fully alert again. It's amazing how one's brain can click right back to life, once you know that rescue is at hand.

"Do you think I should call out yet?"

"No. We're not really in shouting distance yet. Best to wait 'til we've got a bit closer and they can hear us properly."

We start to walk towards them. Yes, they're definitely still coming towards us. *What a stroke of luck!*

Come on, Gordon, don't look too feeble! Try to limp with *some* kind of dignity. Don't act too injured, for God's sake! Don't overdramatise.

John stops.

"They seem to have stopped," he says. "What *are* they doing?"

I stop. "I don't know. Strange."

They're absolutely stationary, just this side of the crest, apparently staring up at us.

"I think they may have spotted us," John says.

"No, I think that's unlikely. I think it's more likely they're scanning the mountainside to see if they can see us."

"Yeah … I think you could be right. Look! – I think Brian's got some binoculars held up to his face."

Could be. But they don't seem to be moving. How odd. Perhaps they're just tourists who've come up here late at night for a bit of sightseeing, and they're going to turn round and go down again any second? That would be a disaster. We've got to attract their attention.

"I think we should call now. Give them a shout," I say.

John cups his hands to his mouth and calls out: "Hello! Hello!" Very far away, his voice echoes back from the far mountainside.

They just keep staring at us. Have they heard us?

"Hello – oh!… oh!… Can you hear us? … hear us? … Can you see us? … see us? … " John waves with his hands.

Still they don't answer. How most peculiar.

They're obviously not going to answer us, so we just keep on walking (and limping) towards them.

John stops again.

"What on earth are they doing?"

It looks like the one on the left has stooped down, and is bending over something. And the guy who looks like Brian is just standing there, watching him.

"I think Hugh's lighting a fire *…* Isn't that smoke I can see?"

There's definitely *something* between them … something murky. Something milky …

"I don't think that's smoke," I opine. Then: "I think they're holding a net," I speculate.

We watch for a while. It's very odd.

"I don't think it's a net," John says. "I think it's a banner or something. And they're holding it up … Maybe for us to see …?"

They do seem to be stretching something filmy out between them now.

"I still think it looks like a net. I'm sure it's a net. *How strange.*"

The left-hand one has his head turned towards us now. "I can see his head moving," I say. "Isn't he looking towards us again?"

John says: "No, I think they've turned their backs on us."

God, if they walk away now, it'll be a real disaster!

"No, hang on! … Brian's definitely looking at us again. I think he just waved, didn't he?"

For some reason we don't feel like calling out again. There seems to be something faintly spastic about doing that.

"Let's go and see what the hell they *are* doing!" John says.

Now, Gordon, for God's sake, when you reach them, don't play "the hero". I know what you've done is pretty bloody heroic, escaping death by the skin of your teeth, and then doing the whole of the rest of the climb with a very badly injured knee – but really try to be modest, don't let it show – really play it down. The thing is just to tell them how grateful we are that they've come, and then let them completely take charge of everything. Just do exactly what they say – it'll be over to them now – they know the route. Just play it all down. Just say something like: "Thanks so much for coming – we really weren't expecting anyone to find us."

Come on Gordon, you're cringing like a Trollkjerringa! Don't look too much of an old woman. Try to stand up a bit.

I notice John's hanging back, keeping alongside me, closer than he's been on the whole descent, almost shepherding me along, obviously a bit embarrassed by the strange way our rescuers are behaving, just staring at us. Obviously he's wanting to present a public face of us being very much a team.

As we near them with mounting excitement, I'm becoming ever

more self-conscious being stared at like this. It's really hard not to look a *bit* like the walking wounded, or something. But I'm trying not to let it show, trying not to let them see that I'm in pain, trying to crawl towards them in as dignified a fashion as possible. And I'm rehearsing what I'm going to say:

"Hi, we really weren't expecting you, it's really great to see you. Thanks a million! It really is a nice surprise, to put it mildly!…" Whatever you do, just don't sound too grand or heroic …

Then John stops. We're just fifteen or twenty feet from them. I stop. We stare.

I sink forward slightly in total disbelief, crumpling, as it were, under the visual impact. I turn a whiter shade of pale.

I might just as well have been hit in the face with a sledgehammer.

We're dead in our boots. The suddenness, the unexpectedness of it is absolutely shocking. As at the horror of yesterday, there are just two images, with no transition. One moment there are two people waiting to greet us, the next they are just two slimy black streaks on the side of a huge muscovite gneiss boulder.

They don't look remotely like people. Just two absolutely straight-sided black water streaks. The flat light from the grey sky is as merciless as mica schist.

It's perhaps the most shocking thing I've ever experienced. The worst moment of all. Because now I know truly, for the first time, just what a very bad way I'm in. We're in broad daylight – at about ten to eleven at night in the land of the midnight sun – and we're losing our senses.

Just how did we imagine those black streaks were *people?* Where have their arms and legs gone? Where are their heads? *What is going wrong with us?* We are quite obviously losing our minds.

John mutters something about it being like waves and particles – but I haven't a clue what he's talking about.

"Sorry? What?… I'm sorry, John, I don't understand what you're saying, I'm just too tired…. Sorry."

I'm trying to fight back the tears, because I know I've got to try to keep a grip. I can't lose control now.

"We have to stop right now," John says, very quietly and firmly. "It's not safe for us to go on. We have to bivvy here and now, while we've still got the strength. We've got to get some sleep, or we've had it. If we carry on there's a real risk we'll fall asleep in the heather and die of exposure. It's as simple as that."

Our emotional gloom can scarcely be exaggerated as we take off our sacks and start to prepare for another miserable night out in the open – in the bitter knowledge that absolutely no one is going to come and rescue us, and that we're going to have to find a way down this steep mountainside in the morning without any help and on the very last reserves of our energy. Not that I have any left now. None whatever.

I'm fighting back the tears of self pity.

I mustn't crack up … I mustn't crack up.

I've never felt quite so dejected, so utterly desolate, so empty, so completely lost. Stuck up on this mountainside still some three thousand feet above the valley floor. In this utterly bleak landscape, this scene without hope.

Neither of us says anything. We're rather like a couple who've just had a flaming row, and aren't speaking to each other any more, as we sullenly prepare for our second night out. I take my damp cagoule out of my sack, and John gets out the crumpled Space Blanket that we'd vowed never to use again. Then we just sit down on the wet grass and heather next to the boulder in our Black's cagoules and pull out the *pied d'elephant* sleeves from our sacks, and put our feet into them, still with our wet and muddy boots on. What an appropriate name that is: I feel about as mobile as a tired old elephant that's been brought to its knees by poisoned darts.

We spread the wretched Space Blanket over ourselves in silence. This ridiculous piece of cellophane, this silver-foil blanket which isn't a blanket.

And then we lie down – right next to the boulder, beside those two damnable black streaks, our "rescuers", like mocking guardian angels that couldn't care a damn.

I feel very cold, and wracked by a thousand aches and pains, but the heathery ground is surprisingly comfortable.

Then I feel something very hard digging into my right thigh. It's the piece of rock I picked up at Ugla Skar. I close my hand round it. A fat lot of good it's done us so far.

In a matter of seconds I hear John snoring, very loudly. My God, he went out like a light. What a din!

And:

Ping, ping, ping, ping, Ping! … goes the hammering in my head, in my temples.

God, I hate this factory.

Now, for the first time in many hours, I can feel myself falling into a tunnel of deepest sleep, falling again – down, down, down, into a bottomless black pit.

ping, ping, ping …

III

TUESDAY

pat …

pat …

pat – pat – pat …

Pat, Pat, Pat, Pat, *Pat!*

I wake with a start, to the heavy patter of raindrops on the Space Blanket. In a few seconds they're exploding loudly off the silver foil in a fusillade. This is obviously not just going to be a gentle shower. I'm already very cold and damp, and it doesn't take me more than a few seconds to realize that we're going to have to get moving immediately, or we're going to be in very serious trouble.

I peep out from under the foil. The cloud has come right down, and I can see very little of the mountain above us.

I prod John in his sack.

"John!"

Nothing. I shake him. He jumps. "Wha – what's going on?"

"It's raining, we've gotta move!"

"What?" groggily.

"John, it's raining really hard."

"Bloody hell, what on earth's the time? … " He looks at his watch … "Christ, we've only been asleep for about half an hour!"

"Yeah, I know, but we're going to get soaked. We've got to move now, or we're going to die of exposure."

Now he's sitting up, wide awake in the rain in his cagoule. "OK. You're right."

He immediately gets out of his sack. I do likewise and hop round in little circles in front of the boulder to try and get the circulation going.

Strangely enough, the boulder with its two black streaks is now ever so slightly reassuring, I don't know why. I suppose it's because it is just a good old solid boulder, and those streaks are *not* guardian angels.

John stuffs the wet Space Blanket back into his sack; does up his bootlaces; and says, "OK?" He has to wait – with the ghastly lifeless wilderness of rock behind him, the weeping clouds above, and the damp wind tugging at us – while I put my nearly empty sack on my back. Then, as the deluge starts in earnest, we set off, staggering like drunkards, having stiffened up after our short rest. John heads straight off down the heathery slope, going in zigzags, working out the best line for me, and I hobble after him. I can hardly see him in the murk.

Actually I'm feeling much more alert after my short kip – and in much higher spirits. It's nice to be moving again, and getting some warmth back into my limbs. All we've got to do now is find the path and get down. That's all. *"That's all"?* Then at last I'll be able to get into my sleeping bag in our cosy tent.

This walking in the rain brings on a touch of the Del Shannons. I can't get it out of my head now. Humming it in snatches, but mostly hearing it in my head:

"… I'm a-walking in the rain,
"Tears are fallin' and I feel the pain,
"A'wishing you were here by me –
"To end this misery,
"And I wonder …
"I wah – wah – wah – wah – wonder!
"Why?
"Why, why, why, why, why she ran away …
"Yes, and I wonder …"

John's waiting for me.

"How's the knee?"

"Completely locked solid, but it's OK. It's holding up." If only there were some trees here and I could find a stick …

About 2.30 am

"I wah – wah – wah – wah – wonder,

"Why?

"Why, why, why, why, why – she ran away …"

– I'm humming now – grabbing roots – a steep step –

"An-and I wonder, a-where she will stay - ay - ay,

"my little runaway …

"a, run, run, run, *run* away! …"

I can hear that orchestral backing screeching now: *wah – wa, wa – wah, wah, wah!* –

I slip. Keep a grip, Gordon! Or you're going to die here …

"I wah – wah – wah – wah – wonder,

"Why?

"Why, why, why, why – " I slip again – I grab another root. Gordon: watch it! Or you're going to lose this. *Concentrate!* You must not damage your knee any further. Just keep with it … because you can get *hur, hur, hurt!*

We've been coming down this ever-steepening slope of wet grass and heather for at least an hour, ever closer to the lip of the hanging valley. The bottom of Isterdal is still hidden tantalisingly from view in a gloomy purple abyss beyond.

The rain has stopped, but the heather is very wet. I'm using my Millar mitts to lower myself now, even though they're soaked through. Earlier, we crossed the fast-flowing stream by a series of flat boulders and rock slabs because the slope on the far side looked less heathery, but now it's got much thicker again and my breeches and snow gaiters are completely saturated. John is deliberately not going too far ahead of me now – just twenty or thirty feet – to make sure I'm OK on this steeper ground. He's always waiting now until the moment I reach him.

We take off our cagoules because we're getting too hot. We're literally steaming. Above us hangs a huge vertical crag, at least fifteen hundred feet high – gashed with enormous clean grooves separated by stupendous arêtes. It would be absolutely covered in famous rock climbs if it was anywhere in the British Isles.

We carry on. We haven't so much as mentioned the mythical "path" for the last hour – it's almost as if it's become a taboo subject, so inexplicable is its nonappearance. The main thing is that we're losing height rapidly, and we're getting off the mountain.

I'm singing out loud now, breathlessly, as I slip and slide:

"I wah-wah-wah-wah-wonder …

"… Why? … " (Very out of breath.)

"Why, why, why, why, why? …

"She ran away! …

"… And I won— " Bur, boomp! –

Bloody hell, *watch it, Gordon!* You've really bruised your bum now.

John has stopped. "I can hear the waterfall," he calls back.

Yes, I can too now. That surely must be Stegfoss. But it's odd … although the ground is getting steeper and steeper, there's *still* no sign of a path anywhere. We're now descending a very steep slope of dense, knee-high bushes, very bright green. They're very springy, and are spraying us with water with every downward step. My needlecord breeches are clinging coldly to my legs, but at least it's keeping my knee chilled. The guidebook, that I've got folded in half in my right-hand pocket, has turned into a soggy wodge of saturated paper, a bit like a slab of damp Kendal Mint Cake … If only!

This is getting silly. The convex slope, poised above the deep trench of Isterdal, is becoming more and more insecure. I'm letting gravity do most of the work. My snow gaiters have got pushed right up and various bits of heather and twigs have got into my boots. But I can't stop to take them off now. At least, very soon, all will be revealed and we'll be able to see Stegfoss at last.

John's gone on ahead a bit: he's walking fast out onto a slight promontory where we'll be able to see right down into the bottom of the valley. The moment of truth is drawing near.

I think I hear an exclamation. John turns to look at me. "You're not going to like this," he says.

In a couple of minutes I reach him. I look.

I'm looking straight into Isterdal.

It's that sledgehammer of shock again. It's so utterly different from how I expected it to be.

Desolation reigns. There's not a sign of life, not a human habitation to be seen. The only suggestion that man has ever been in this huge, primeval U-shaped trench of a valley is a minute little road, perhaps two thousand feet below, running alongside the river at the bottom – so small that it could be a single track affair, as in the highlands of Scotland. With huge rock walls and wet slabs towering above it, it's like Romsdal but without any human habitation.

But that's not the worst of it. We are looking at the valley floor through empty space: there is apparently a huge line of crags directly beneath us. And, to our right, a gargantuan slab of smooth rock tilts over the abyss like the roof of a house, with giant steps in it instead of tiles and, down the middle, three huge torrents thunder down it, to disappear over a jagged edge. If this is the waterfall of Stegfoss – which now seems extremely unlikely – there's no "viewing place above the waterfalls" of any kind, and not a single building by the road below.

X marks the spot where our first attempt to descend into Isterdal comes to an abrupt halt

Worse still, there's no trace of a footpath anywhere to be seen – indeed, there's no evidence whatever that anyone's ever been on this mountainside. Ever. The blunt fact that we have to face up to is that there is obviously no feasible direct route into Isterdal this way.

It's a very serious turn of events; and John's looking very drawn. "We're just going to have to go back up," he says quietly, "and find the proper route." He's adamant, yet I can't see much conviction in his face.

"Do you think," I dare to suggest, "it's somewhere completely different?"

"I dunno. But it really doesn't matter a damn now. We've just got to find a route that works."

"Perhaps," I suggest, "we can find a way that skirts round the mountainside to our right somewhere?"

We've no choice, then, but to head up to where the angle eases, and see if we can find such an alternative. It's our only hope. And, like so many of the psychological blows we've experienced already, it has its own consequent nightmare: we now have to claw our way back up this horrible steep, slippery slope for many hundreds of feet.

Our mood is as sombre as our surroundings. I take off my Millar mitts and wring them out. My hands are all wrinkly with the damp, and there's pus coming out of the cracks round my fingernails. I take off my boots, empty out the bits of gravel and heather, and ring out my socks. I won't describe the smell. At least, if the pain in my knee gets worse, and I'm in need of an effective anaesthetic, all I'll have to do is clamp one of my boots over my face like a gas mask.

A little voice is screaming within me: *it's our own bloody fault!* We didn't find out about the descent route before we set off. We didn't do our homework. I have that same ghastly apprehension now that I felt so often in our School Chapel in the morning, knowing that I'm heading for disaster because I haven't done my Prep – and that in an hour or two I'm going to be found out when I flunk a crucial test. My worst experience was a test I once had that involved reading a passage in Greek and then answering (all in Greek) a series of fiendish questions relating to it. I couldn't answer a single one: yes, it was "all Greek to me". Well, I guessed one or two, and answered in plain English. I felt like adding one or two good old Anglo-Saxon expletives, but refrained. When I got the test back, the following week I found that the Greek master, Mr Smedley-Jones (whom I loathed – I think it was mutual), had inscribed a terrifying legend across the top, in his very neat, scholarly handwriting:

He didn't write it in the usual way: 0/20, but put the nought very neatly in the middle, on top of the twenty. And underneath it, carefully centred:

Ignorant? – – Or bone idle??

Just like that, with those two dashes and three dreadful question marks. And then I had to take it to the headmaster – the "Arch", as we used to call him – Mr McCrum (actually we called him "Crud", but that is another matter), and he demanded of me:

"Well, which is it, Stainforth?"

There was only one answer, of course, and I had to get it right first time.

"Bone idle, sir!" I squeaked (correctly). But it didn't help, because I was beaten for it all the same: four strokes of the cane. I kid you not. And very painful it was too …

We're being caned now. The bad dream continues.

Zero hour

We've dragged ourselves up about six or seven hundred feet, perhaps even further, back up the slope of miniature bushes, and Store Trolltind has truly become Mount Purgatory. I have scarcely an ounce of energy left in me. I don't know what I'm actually running on now, but it ain't food. Sheer will, I suppose, combined with a deep, ever-increasing fear that this is not going to turn out all right, and the Big Troll is going to get us in the end.

It's so physically gruelling that the only way I can cope with it – psychologically – is by doing nothing else but count down from a hundred, over and over again:

"… ninety-nine, ninety-eight, ninety-seven, ninety-six, ninety-five, ninety-four …"

My body is now in all-out rebellion. My legs have just about given up, so my arms are having to do much more than their fair share. Actually, this isn't Purgatory, it's sheer Hell.

We're out of the wet bushes now, and crawling more or less on our hands and knees – heaving ourselves up on tufts of grass and heather. Even John. He's not more than twenty feet above me, and going very slowly indeed. If anything, this heather slope is even more arduous than the bushes. At least, there, I could pull myself up with my arms, but now I'm forced to use my legs much more, or rather, my knees. (I won't mention the pain). So, while it's not very steep, I would describe it as "a killer incline", being set at the worst possible angle for both arms and legs – and it's utterly relentless.

"… Forty-six, forty-five, forty-four, forty-three, forty-two, forty-one, forty, thirty-nine …"

I am absolutely soaked, and covered in dirt and twigs; and my thighs have all the vigour of soggy balsawood. The angle is easing still further, but we are going ever more slowly. I'm having to stop every thirty feet or so – for longer and longer rests.

"… ten, nine, eight, seven, six, five, four, three, two, one, zero …"

And we have not got lift-off; we have got zero. So I have no choice but to go back to the beginning, back to the very top, the full ton:

"Ninety-nine, ninety-eight, ninety-seven, ninety-six …"

The slope is falling right back as we come over the lip of the hanging valley on all fours. Now I'm stopping every ten feet. I'm so tired my eyelids are drooping.

What did I do to deserve this? You were stupid, Gordon! … Very stupid; and ignorant, and – – bone idle. I'm so idle now, I'm hardly moving. I can't put any more effort into it, because there's none to give. We really have become snails at last.

There's another slight steepening ahead, so that I can't see anything beyond, except John, only about fifteen feet in front of me, having almost as much trouble as I am. I use my hands again on tufts of heather to heave myself up onto a gentler terrace, and lean forward, gasping, my heart thumping …

… And I realize to my utter horror that *I can no longer take a single step further forward*.

There is absolutely nothing left in me: my fuel gauge is on empty, my tank is dry. I am, in effect, pinned to the ground by gravity and my total powerlessness to do anything about it. I'm quite literally stuck. My body won't do it; it's simply packed up and said, That's it, mate, I'm finished!

It's a terrifying moment, one of the most terrifying things I've ever experienced – worse even than falling off.

I glance up to see how John is faring. He's only about ten feet in front of me and, like myself, is frozen absolutely static, slumped forward in the heather in an identical position to myself. The identical twins.

"John … ?"

"I can't go any further. I've had it."

"Nor can I."

We have both ground to a halt at precisely the same moment, forming a frozen tableau with a dramatic mountain background.

A dramatic mountain background? It's an entirely new background: a broad vista of high, snowy mountains standing proud against an overcast sky.

The cloud has lifted at last. For the very first time we can see the distant skyline of a huge mountain – Breitind, I think – at the head of the hanging valley. And big snowfields.

"Jesus!"

John is gazing up at the distant scene as if he's seen an apparition.

"Can you see that?"

I look. Yes – yes, unfortunately I can. *Oh, shit!* Oh big shit. Oh very big shit.

At the far end of the hanging valley, perhaps two miles away and two thousand feet above us, going straight across a very obvious snowfield, there's a faint but distinct horizontal line. And at regular intervals along it – confirming its true status for us – there are several small, dark triangular points. I'm afraid they can't be anything else: they're obviously cairns. The mystery of the "Ordinary Route" is solved at last, and we're absurdly far from it. The real descent route has never come down this hanging valley at all; and now it's completely unattainable. Even if we could be magically levitated to that distant furrow in the snow, it would be no good to us, because it's far too high and far too cold. We wouldn't last more than a few minutes up there above the snowline in our present condition.

Where, then, is the elusive Stegfoss? It must be somewhere far to our south, beyond an intervening ridge. It's not in Isterdal at all. It's miles away, in a completely different direction. Exactly where is totally irrelevant now. We can't get there. The reason we couldn't find it on the map is that it's almost certainly off the map. That's why. It's a very sick joke indeed. And the enormous distance we are from it pummels home the full gravity of our mistake – gravity being something we've learnt rather a lot about in the last three days. My life could – seriously – now do with a touch of levity.

"My God, we've screwed up big time," says John, pursing his cracked lips and frowning deeply.

We have a near-monosyllabic consultation, the most serious in our lives. If we don't manage to find a route down, this is where we will stay. We *have* to force a way down this impossible-looking mountainside, or we're finished. If we fail to find a route we're facing certain death for the second time in just two days. In some ways, dying like this is even worse than falling, because it's likely to be a long drawn out process of gradual deterioration until we're too weak to move any further in any direction, even downwards.

All the time during this grim review, I'm chewing pieces of

moss, and spitting them out, but at least John's no longer making any comments about my new feeding habits.

What to do? We can't go up because it's no longer physically possible. We can't go down because it's too technically difficult. We can only go sideways. But we can't go north because that direction is blocked by the giant waterfall we saw earlier, and the huge crag beyond it. The only possibility is southwards – to our left, facing out. If we can't find a weakness that way, there's now no question about it: we've had it.

What happens if we can't? We'll just have to abseil. Neither of us mentions the subject of only having two knifeblade pegs.

There are no other options left. It's our very last chance.

I clasp the "lucky" stone in my pocket very firmly.

Sometime in the great somewhere.

And now an extraordinary thing has happened to us: we have clicked into a completely new state – a state that is essential for our further existence. It isn't simply that we have found a second wind: this is our final wind and we know it. Suddenly we're more alert than we've ever been in our lives, more focused than at any point on the entire route. It's as if a cloud has cleared in my head, and I suddenly can see everything with total clarity. I think a lot of it is to do with being twins. We are quite literally thinking as one now, making every decision in unison – much of the time not verbalizing it at all. If one of us calls out "left" or "down", it is simply an expression of what we are jointly thinking: an announcement rather than a command. And it's all completely monosyllabic.

"Left …"

"Left …"

"Down …"

"Yes …"

"Left …"

The English public school accents are strangely out of place in this barren Norwegian wasteland, and the words are often many minutes apart. There are no longer any extraneous voices going on in my head, nothing except the task of thinking where to place my feet and where the route goes next. We are taking a completely different line on this second and last attempt. Always we are moving leftwards, but with gravity – and the underlying "dip" of the rock – pulling us slightly down to the right. This is the way the mountain is telling us to go now. Or is it luring us into a trap? Only time will tell.

One welcome surprise is that, although we're unable to go uphill, we can still go downhill with little difficulty. In other words, gravity is on our side now. Though I am, of course, taking enormous care, because I'm swaying with fatigue, and my balance isn't so good. We never lose height until we're sure we can link up with another horizontal sloping terrace or weakness of sorts. As long as we're descending – even very slightly – and without technical difficulty, it doesn't matter; all that matters is that we are descending, nearer and nearer to safety.

"Down."

"Left."

"Left" – across ever steeper grassy terraces. When a terrace runs out, we look for a vertical runnel and go down that. We each have six old hemp waistlines in our sacks for use as abseil slings, and John has now developed a new technique of using them as "fixed ropes", which he attaches to bushes and saplings. We're each wearing a Dachstein mitt on our right hand and are lowering ourselves on the quarter-inch line with a twist round our wrists. It's a strange variety of abseiling, really. You just lean backwards slightly and "walk" down the grassy runnel letting gravity do all the work. The point is, we don't want to start real abseiling with the rope a moment sooner than we have to, because that will be immensely time-consuming, and our sands are running out.

My left hand, without a glove, uses what little holds there are – nasty rotten flakes and spikes and so on; and sometimes I simply bury my fingers deep into wet, gravelly earth.

Be very careful with those foot placements, Gordon; be very careful with this gravity thing!…

Sometimes I add one of my own hemp lines for extra safety, where John hasn't bothered.

"Back right …"

"Down."

The route gets harder and harder as we approach a sweep of unbroken slabs. Soon we're making our way along vegetated ledge systems and horizontal lines of weakness in the slabs, their smoothness below us heightening the sense of exposure; and before long, we are making our way across ledges and flakes, almost rock climbing.

Here we get a glimpse of the lonely road again. There's no sign of any cars. So if we become stuck (or unstuck) – even if we had torches to flash – there's no one around to see them. And even if there was, and we had a mirror, the chances of attracting anyone's attention in broad daylight are precisely zilch. It would be about as much use as waving a handkerchief in the middle of the Atlantic Ocean.

"Left …"

"Left …"

La la, life goes on.

It's around "breakfast time" (Ha, ha) …

… And our luck has run out completely. We are surrounded by smooth slabs. It's the end of our road to freedom.

About eighty feet below us, the slab ends abruptly at a sharp edge, and there's nothing beyond it except the immense trench of Isterdal about a thousand feet below. If our side of the valley below these overhangs is anything like the huge slabs and overhangs we can see the other side, we are doomed. And, sadly, there is no way we can traverse any further; beyond the smooth slab we are on there are enormous rock buttresses full of overhangs. The only way is down. We're going to have to abseil. But we are obviously going to have to get much nearer the lip of the overhang first, because the chances of ending up in space on the end of the rope seem rather high.

The only feature on the slab below us is a narrow ledge covered in small saplings, about fifty feet below.

"That is going to have to be our abseil point," John says, verbalizing my thought. Nothing else is said. We don't discuss the rather momentous question of how many overhangs may lie below, and just how many abseils we may have to make with our very limited supply of pegs. We know that we are in last chance saloon, basically.

There is a small bush next to us to tie a hemp waistline to, but unfortunately, as soon as John tugs at it, it virtually comes away in his hand. Clearly an avalanche has swept down here very recently at the end of the winter, and almost pulled it from its roots. But there is a good crack in the rock and, without a word, John inserts one of our metal wedges, and attaches a hemp line to it.

As he works his way down a runnel in the slab, using the hemp line as a fixed rope, I feel curiously calm. We are absolutely in the hands of the gods now – or the Trolls, and there's nothing whatever that we can do about it. If it doesn't work out, we'll die – but at least we tried.

I'm not even bothering to watch John now; I'm just gazing across the valley at the hideous mile-high fortress of Kongen – "The King", featuring some of the biggest overhangs I've ever seen. A completely mad, grotesquely upscaled, Nordic version of King Lear made out of granitic schist, gazing down on the childish antics of the Stainforth Fools.

When John reaches the end of the hemp line, he heaves himself into balance and attaches a second length to it; then carries on down. And when that runs out, he simply sits on his bum and climbs directly down to the ledge facing outwards. As I say, I'm watching it all in a very disinterested manner, as if I'm watching a movie and it's not really happening to me.

Tony Howard, in the guidebook, says these are "some of the most beautiful mountains in Europe". Well, frankly, I've never seen anything quite so ugly or repulsive as Kongen.

"OK!" John's voice rings out in the silence of the morning. "Come on."

"Are there any anchor points?"

"I'm looking – but come on." Well, I suppose that's logical enough. There's no point in me staying up here, even if there are no abseil points; we might as well die together.

I climb down using the hemp line in a bit of a trance, somehow not caring too much. If we can't abseil from here, it's all over. We've let the side down. We're failures. It's as simple as that. Sod's Law.

I slowly climb down the last bit on my bum. John's just sitting on the ledge in his fetid blue anorak gazing at Kongen. He turns to me rather bleary-eyed. (Is it possible he's been sleeping?).

"There aren't any peg placements," he says. "Nothing."

"Come on, John! We've got to find something. It's our last chance!"

The ledge John's sitting on is about ten feet long – about a foot wide at our end, but tapering to nothing at the other. Very conveniently, just above it at chest level there's another narrow ledge, covered in very small saplings. I know they look absurdly flimsy, but surely John has tried to see if any is strong enough to take our weight? Apparently not.

I grab the one nearest to me and give it a violent shake. Oh God, it's completely useless. It's just loosely stuck in the earth at the back of the ledge. I grab the next one. Just the same. It's obvious that huge avalanches have come down this slab at the end of the winter and have more or less torn out all the saplings. Perhaps there are still one or two that are adequate? There's a profusion of them, as many as four dozen, all about the diameter of a finger, and we must test each one of them systematically.

I seem to be taking charge now that John has become a complete zombie. I tell him that I'll go to the left end of the ledge and we'll work our way towards each other, testing them one by one.

My heart sinks as I work my way back towards John, tugging at each finger-width sapling. They're all just the same, all far too flimsily attached to the ledge to bear our weight. Closer and closer we get to each other, until there's just one left. We happen to put our hands on it at the very same moment, and – quite miraculously (the word is not too strong) – it's dead solid. The only one. It's about the diameter of a thumb, but more than adequate. So now that we have an anchor point, all we have to do is get the rope ready …

Time stands still

We're in slow motion, trying to untangle the damp rope. Only our hands are moving. Neither of us is saying anything. We're simply too tired to speak. John merely heaves an occasional very deep sigh; other times he just gives a fierce little sniff through his nose.

We've been doing this for at least half an hour, and the end of it is nowhere in sight. Almost the more we do to try and unravel the rope, the more tangled it seems to get. It really is the very last straw. (Well, we know that, don't we?)

When John got the rope out of his sack, we were dumbfounded by the state it was in. I've certainly never seen a worse tangle. John said he was lying on it for insulation last night … but I don't see how that has tangled it. It's just another of those inexplicable Trolltind mysteries that we have become so used to now.

Patience, patience. At some point in history we'll reach the end of the rope, and it will be completely untangled. Rather like the mysteries of life.

We've got a sort of system going whereby John's threading and unthreading bits of it, and pulling other bits, while I feed him yet other bits, and keep the whole tangled mass as loose as possible.

Did I say "system"? No, that's the wrong word! There's no system at all here that even the most intelligent observer could discern. Actually, the technical trick now I've resorted to is good old-fashioned prayer, because I've threatened to become a Buddhist if this doesn't work out. That means I'll end my last hours on this ledge sitting cross-legged. Not sure what happens at the Pearly Gates, though. Perhaps they don't have any Pearly Gates?

There's a sense that the sun's trying to come through the cloud, and it's a lot warmer, so I'm now very drowsy indeed. I'm right on the edge of sleep …

John suddenly says:

"You do realize it's Dad's birthday today?" – in a very flat tone, apropos of nothing. Except everything.

"No, I'd completely forgotten."

We lapse into silence again. I hope we will not be giving him the worst birthday present he's ever had.

Suddenly the whole rope simply falls apart, all completely untangled – so easily I'm almost annoyed with it. What was all that about, then? Sulking like that? It's just lying there looking so innocent now, in neat coils, all ready for work. OK, we won't make an issue of it.

John feeds the red end of the rope through the nylon tape sling we've put round the sapling, while I pay it out. He stops at the half way point, where it turns to yellow. Then he picks up the two ends and ties them together with a huge double figure-of-eight knot. That's to stop me going off the end of the rope, if I'm left hanging in space. I'm going first, by the way, though we haven't discussed it yet. It's a standard procedure for the strongest man to come down last, because he's in a position to help the first man. The last man down on an abseil can't be helped at all from above (or from below) if anything goes wrong.

Now we get out our long tape slings, twist them into figures-of-eight, and step into the two "holes". Then we reach down between our legs, pull up the point where the sling crosses over and clip them into our waist karabiners.

We're all ready.

I break the long silence.

"I'll go first then – OK?"

"Yes. Fine."

Of course, to a non-climber it may seem very "brave" of me to be going first but, actually, John has the gutsier job of being left behind, and having to wait and wonder, once I've disappeared over the lip of the overhang.

One possible problem – of many! – is that I may not be able to see immediately what our prospects are. There could be a series of overhangs to go over before I can find out if there's a possible way down. If I get into real trouble, and I find myself hanging in space on the end of the rope, John will be faced with the fate of being stranded up here for ever, just tied to that sapling on a sheet of slabs in a very inaccessible place on a rather remote mountain in Norway.

I take off my sack, because it could interfere with my abseil ropes – and we need to give this the best possible chance. John clips it to the anchor point, so that it won't be dropped (not that it's got anything very useful in it now … not even a prayer book. Forgot that.) If the first abseil goes well, he's then going to have to lower both sacks to me, before he can abseil himself. John hands me the bandolier with all seven pegs.

Now I get hold of the two ropes and clip them into my waist karabiner. I do up the screwgate very firmly. Then I bring the ropes up over my left shoulder, and down across my back and into my right hand. Taking the world, as it were, upon my shoulder.

I have a final check that my screwgate is done up properly; check that the ropes are nestled in nicely around my turned-up anorak hood; and flick the ropes below me to check that they feel free, and aren't snagged on anything.

I don't tell John, but they feel very heavy, which means that they're hanging in space beyond the overhang. Better not to tell him yet another piece of bad news.

Very careful now. Double-check everything. Quadruple-check everything. This is your last chance.

There's no point now in putting off the moment of truth any longer. When I get to the lip of the overhang our fate will almost certainly be revealed.

I step down below John, taking most of my weight on my feet

on the slab. It's very painful on my left leg, but so what? My life depends now on abseiling properly, in the conventional manner.

Holding the ropes going up to the anchor point in my left hand, I lean back, very gently. The sapling bends slightly as my weight comes onto it, then a bit more as I put my full weight on it. But it doesn't bend any more. It's OK. Then I let the ropes slide a bit through my right hand until I'm leaning backwards at right angles to the slab.

It's what they call a suspenseful moment – suspended by two strands of coloured nylon, with only fate and gravity to help me now. Stiff upper lip.

"OK, I'm going," I say. I nearly said "I'm off" – that wouldn't have been very fortunate, would it?

"OK. Good luck!" John's deliberately not showing any emotion at all.

Gently does it, Gordon, don't rush … I start to "walk" backwards down the smooth slab very slowly and carefully, so as not to make the slightest jerk on the sapling. Also, it's very important to make sure I'm keeping the ropes going in the correct position around the side of my neck. If it slips off my shoulder I'll plunge down the full length of the 150-foot ropes to almost certain death.

I glance up at the diminishing figure of my brother, who is understandably looking very anxious. He already seems quite far away, and very lonely indeed. There's a possibility we may never see each other again.

As I near the lip, tension mounts even higher, if that's possible. Yes, I can report that it is.

I keep walking down very slowly and smoothly until the toes of my boots are right on the very lip of the overhang. The ropes feel very heavy, digging into my shoulder. The moment of truth. I say a little prayer to myself.

I look down.

It's a moment I'll never forget as long as I live. Life divided into two: the "before" and "after" this moment.

I almost gasp out loud. It's just so different from what I was expecting.

I'm on the edge of a huge overhang, looking straight down the ropes – which are hanging clean through space – and, at the very bottom –

– the last eighteen inches of the ropes are lying neatly curled up on a flat grassy ledge, like a little basking dog. And, below that, a very steep densely-clad mountainside of luxuriant green birch trees comes roaring straight up towards me to end just below the ledge. There's no other way to describe it: it's another drop that roars – but this one in a very different way. A roar of friendship. Because, almost directly below me, a huge shallow rocky gully, full of boulders, cuts a great swathe down through the trees, all the way down to the lonely road at the bottom, almost a thousand feet below. A royal road through the trees … a road to freedom. In this instant – just one glance – I know that we are saved.

I really can't keep back the tears now. I'm choking, I can hardly say the words, as I look back up at John:

"It's OK, John! … *It's OK!*"

"Really? Are you sure?"

"Yes." Crying. Just sticking both thumbs up, even though I've got ropes in both hands, jabbing them in unison, quite unable to speak.

When I've pulled myself together a bit, I say weakly:

"OK, I'm going down now," and I simply step off the edge of the overhang into space.

The ropes whack against the lip of the slab – I'm afraid it's a bit of a jerk on the sapling – but I'm still hanging there. Then I just let the ropes slide gently through my hands, and I'm spinning slowly round, rotating, now facing dear old, friendly Kongen – beautiful Kongen! – and now coming right around again to face the rock.

It's rather lovely. I just couldn't care a damn about anything anymore. I'm blissfully happy. Levity. Amazing grace! I was stuck, and now I'm free. Just sliding gently back down to earth, back to the world. Everything.

Crying with joy, now.

Down, down, down I go – down and down – round and round –

until my toes touch the ground and I alight on the grassy terrace.

I quickly undo the screwgate of my karabiner and unclip the red and orange ropes. And I say to myself: what a wonderful world!

At the eleventh hour

We're now deep in the woods, a long way below the overhanging wall we abseiled down. There were some steep little walls below the terrace that weren't obvious from above, and eventually we were forced leftwards into the woods where we could use branches and tree roots to help overcome the steeper steps. In other words, it wasn't quite as easy as we were expecting, but the angle's easing a bit now, and quite frankly I couldn't care a damn.

Also, retrieving the sacks and rope was much more difficult than we'd imagined. It can only be described as one hell of a palaver. Both sacks jammed on the lip of the overhang, and we had to set up a complicated back-rope system, with me flicking the rope from below to help free them. It was well over an hour before John joined me.

Now we're just ploughing down through the very steep, almost impenetrable wood, letting gravity do most of the work, sliding down through a complex lattice of branches, and getting absolutely drenched with water spray. It's not technically difficult, just very awkward, involving lots of backbreaking contortionist moves under very low branches, which would be fine for an able-bodied person. But, for me, with my locked-in-a-right-angle knee, it's very tricky indeed, and John's having to wait ages for me at every obstacle. And it's nothing but obstacles.

My ice axe on the back of my sack is catching all the time on the branches, which means that at least I'm not going to fall very far if I slip. But, really, you may be surprised to know that just about all I am thinking is: Isn't it good, Norwegian wood? I'd almost hum it, if I wasn't so tired.

Now we come to a taller, mossy rock wall, about fifteen feet high. There are big tree roots all over it, and John shins down in a moment; but it's all far too difficult for me. I simply open my sack, get out my big orange tape sling, and tie it round a sturdy tree root. It's not nearly long enough, so I add another old grey tape sling to it, and just slither down, using it as a kind of fixed rope.

I don't normally like the idea of leaving any litter in the mountains – anywhere – but of this, I'll have to say, I'm rather proud. It's a solitary memento of our passing. I wonder just how long it'll stay here. Decades? Hundreds of years? It'll be a complete mystery to anyone who ever finds it. Why on earth was anyone ever up here in this very peculiar place on this mountainside, so far off any recognised or conceivable route? It also feels a bit like an offering to the Trolls, in thanks for our release.

Lower down we come to another wall, not so big as the first, and I abandon another expensive nylon sling in the same way. Then the wood thins out and I can see glimpses of the rock gully again on our right. John goes ahead and finds a small hole through the bushes. I follow, but get delayed by the sight of some beautiful pale pink mountain flowers, orchids I think they're called. I suppose some people might say they're just weeds, but right now, to me, they're the most beautiful things I've ever seen.

And then we are out into the rock gully, on big rough slabs covered with enormous, precariously perched boulders. Most of them are so critically poised that, if you were careless, you could bring one down on top of you, and be crushed, but after all that we've experienced they don't bother us a bit. It's a walk in the park, "beyond all difficulties", to use an expression much beloved of climbing guidebook writers.

It's now so relatively easy that there's no need for John to watch me any longer. He just turns round and says "it's very easy rock steps", and forges on ahead. I'm still going very slowly, taking care with every step, using my hands as much as possible to take the weight off my poor old left knee.

I hear a happy cry and, far below, I see John at a gap in the trees with a glimpse of tarmac beyond. He goes through the gap and disappears. At which precise moment, the sun comes out.

And so, for a short while I am left alone, crawling almost on all fours down some sunny rock slabs on the side of Store Trolltind, a mountain I shall not be visiting again any time soon.

12.15 pm

My feet drop down a short grassy bank onto horizontal tarmac. It has all the satisfaction of scoring a bull's eye at darts or winning the football pools. What strange stuff this tarmac seems – but oh, oh, so lovely. Much nicer than any gneiss that's ever been invented.

John is so quiet that for a moment I don't see him. He's slumped back in the grassy bank, surrounded by his helmet and sack on one side and a great pile of tangled rope on the other. Which now looks more like a great pile of brown dung than a climbing rope. All steaming in the gentle sun.

He scarcely says anything. He just turns to look at me, his tired eyes full of quiet joy. Gaunt is a totally inadequate word to describe the way he looks. I don't think I've really looked at his face properly for about two days. His cheeks are completely sunken, and his skin is weatherbeaten and flushed, like an old seafarer. And he has great, sore, cracked lips and staring eyes, as if he's seen a ghost. His eyes are somehow much too large for his head, so shrunken and emaciated is his face. Emaciated. That's the word.

I probably look even worse.

I throw my sack onto the bank next to him and slump backwards in the soft grass. I'm too tired even to take my boots off. Normally it's about the first thing I'd do. But I'd rather leave them on now, until I get to some soap and water, because I know the smell will be quite horrendous.

Almost casually, I turn my attention to my knee. The breeches and the adhesive bandage have been pushed right up again, exposing the injury in all it's garish glory. The colours are even more livid than when I last looked at it at Ugla Skar (which really seems like a lifetime ago). It's as if Jackson Pollack has done one of his abstract paintings on the side of a beach ball. The adhesive bandage, pushed right up above my knee, is all torn and blotchy with blood stains, and another piece of ordinary bandage has flopped down in a long loop over my socks.

But I really can't be bothered to do anything with it now; that will have to wait for another day. I simply pull the damp bandages back still further, to give it some more air. It seems like a good idea.

It's very quiet. I have my eyes shut now. There's just the sound of many streams and the buzz of a little bee somewhere behind me in the bank.

There's absolutely not a thought in my head. Nothing matters any more. Except that we are here, and we are safe, and we are alive. I dimly realize that, sooner or later – one day, some time – someone is going to come along this road. It could be minutes, it could be hours. We've only seen one car on the road in all the time since the abseil. And that was over two hours ago, shortly after we retrieved the rope. I haven't noticed any since. What we just mustn't do on any account is fall asleep, or any car going past may not realize we're in urgent need of a lift. They might think we're having a deliberate rest – you know, waiting here for friends to pick us up or something.

We've learned a lot about patience in the last three days, so I can easily wait a little bit longer.

I'm just enjoying the warmth of the sun on my skin. It's the nearest thing to meditation I've ever experienced. And, in my pocket, my hand is clutching the rock that I've brought all the way down from Ugla Skar. It's very special to me. I shall treasure it all my life.

In the bank behind me I can hear the little bee, languidly going from flower to flower.

Time future

I can hear another bee now. A very faint hum, so faint that I could almost be imagining it. Now a little bit louder, now fainter again. Miles and miles away.

It's quite musical. A gentle drone that occasionally changes pitch. It's very soothing and peaceful. A distant bee, going about its business …

… But surely it's a very mechanical bee? … Because that is surely an internal combustion engine. That is definitely a car or a van or something, going round various bends, it seems. Something quite small, a very long way away. And I think it's coming our way.

"Can you hear that?" John says.

"Yes."

John is sitting, head forward, listening.

Now the engine sound is much more distinct and coming straight towards us. Then it fades again. Obviously another bend. John gets slowly to his feet. He steps forward onto the tarmac.

And now the car comes hurtling round the corner, about three hundred yards away. Going very fast. A very small car. John sticks his thumb out. It's cream-coloured – a Saab, I think.

It zooms past us, the driver looking straight ahead in an apparent dream, seeming not to notice us at all.

The sound fades to nothing. There's dead silence.

Oh, dear, this could take a very long time. I wonder just how many cars are going to pass us before one stops? Oh well, we're very used to disappointments now.

Suddenly there's another sound, very different, a different engine – very high-pitched, coming in the other direction.

Then the realization: it's the same engine, in reverse. A shrill, high speed whine, in an urgent crescendo.

I glance up at John. His eyebrows have flicked skywards like roller blinds, his eyes wide with astonishment.

Then the Saab comes shooting back round the corner so fast that it's almost out of control. I've never seen a car being driven so fast in reverse.

It screams towards us, weaving slightly, then whips across the road onto the grass verge on the opposite side, and slams to halt with consummate panache.

A hand slides back the window. An anxious face looks out. A flurry of Norwegian, a question. He's looking at my knee.

"We're English," John says.

Straight back, in a strong Norwegian accent:

"Do you need help?"

It's all over, and a new life can begin.

On the summit of Store Vengetind, just two and a half weeks after our Fiva epic.
Right: Gordon; Overleaf: John

AFTERWORD
by
John Stainforth

Looking back across forty years, my mind boggles slightly at how fanatical we'd become about climbing by the time we'd reached the age of nineteen. When we couldn't get to rock, we would be charging round the local parks climbing every tree that offered a technical challenge, whilst dreaming up the next adventure. And when we got to Romsdal our impetuousness was such that we made two huge mistakes even before we had set off on the climb. Firstly, we didn't bother to stock up with adequate food (because it was very inconvenient to go to Åndalsnes, which was in the *opposite* direction to the mountains!) And secondly, though the weather was bad we were so determined to get on the rock that we chose the Fiva Route because we'd been told that it was technically not too difficult. We made the classic youthful error of confusing a lack of great technical difficulty with a lack of seriousness. And, although we railed against the guidebook, as Gordon has described so fully, we completely ignored its warnings about the seriousness of the route on account of its great length and difficult route-finding. We picked the Fiva Route with about as much diligence as choosing a relatively easy climb on a small cliff in North Wales for a poor weather day.

Worse, my snow and ice technique was virtually non-existent, since I had only kicked steps up one or two easy snow slopes in the Alps. Although I had no knowledge of snow and ice types and quality, any fool could see that the snow and ice conditions in the main gully that Gordon led on the route were absolute crap. I knew this in the same way that a newcomer to wine knows that cheap plonk that has gone off really shouldn't be drunk.

Gordon had made my task of seconding up this gully pretty easy. There was his line of cut steps, which had been pressed down by his weight. I had on my Dachstein mitts, and my small ice hammer in my left hand. I found that by punching my fists into the steps I could almost trot up his line of holds. I saw no point in going slowly: we should get up this hazardous terrain as quickly as possible. So I just came up as fast as I could, and was almost certainly going too aggressively on such a delicate surface.

Gordon was taking in the rope somewhat sporadically, possibly because he was tired, and I was climbing so fast he could scarcely take the rope in fast enough. So, frequently, as I was seconding that couloir, I had slack rope alongside my legs or down near my boots. That was how the rope was when the ice around me failed about thirty feet below him. The piece of surface crust that broke off spanned my body from the handholds down to below my feet. It broke away so suddenly and unexpectedly that I didn't have time to think or even curse.

Of course, I was utterly surprised not to be held by the rope and it didn't cross my mind that Gordon had lost control of it. My instantaneous thought was that my waist knot had somehow come untied and that I was simply falling off the ends of the rope. From the instant I shot off downhill, I was completely unaware of the presence of the rope. Instinctively I brought my right hand on top of the ice hammer in my left, which should have been the ideal position to brake my fall, but the small pick made not the slightest impression on the peculiar icy crust of the soft snow. Within a split second it felt as though I weighed ounces, with virtually no weight between me and the slope at all. The act of pushing down with my forearms on the pick may even have pushed me away from the slope, so I was bouncing a foot or so from it. I felt not the slightest resistance of any kind to my fall. There was just this incredible sense of acceleration (in marked contrast to a rock climbing fall) – 0 to 60 mph in a few seconds.

For the first second or so I was swamped with a sense of pure horror, and when I realized I was falling to my certain death, the fear and horror evaporated to be replaced immediately by this enormous sense of guilt, exactly as Gordon experienced it. All I felt was the suck of gravity and did not sense I was moving on to another place; more like the lights going out. Neither did I feel any jerk when I came to the end of the ropes and plucked Gordon off the mountain: if there was a jerk, the circuit breakers of my nervous system had been pulled so completely that I did not feel it.

Nor do I have any recollection of the sensation of being brought to a halt. One minute I was falling free, the next I found myself completely stationary, a few feet down in a gloomy cavity that was several feet across. It was a miracle that I went straight into that minute crevasse, which was only about six inches wide at the surface and probably the only one in the entire couloir. My body must have scored a bull's-eye, feet first.

For a split second I thought: am I dead? And then realized that I was surrounded by very real snow and dripping water. I was completely wrapped in many turns of rope even though I don't think I had spun at all as I fell. The rope must have done a weird kind of Indian Rope trick in reverse, falling vertically down around me in spirals as I shot into the crevasse. For that to happen, I think Gordon must have been flying over my head the instant I went into the crevasse.

I could see in the gloom this great bird's nest of rope jammed up against the downhill wall of the crevasse, alongside my left shoulder. I found there was tension on the center of the bundle of rope and I grabbed a loop from near there and quickly tied it back into my waist karabiner. This is when I saw that I was still properly tied onto the ends of the rope: knots or karabiners had not come undone. This micro-crevasse was actually an amazingly good natural belay spot and I was probably as safe in there as in a tank.

I unwound myself from the rope, lifting some coils over my head. Then I pulled up awkwardly on the downhill side of the crevasse and poked my head out of the six-inch slot: and was very surprised to see Gordon about thirty feet below me, squatting, facing out. Up to then, I thought I had fallen on my own leaving him stranded at his belay. When he turned round and said in disbelief 'Are you alive?' I didn't realize that my head, with neck flush with the snow, looked like John the Baptist's on a platter. A strand of rope, in mild tension, ran straight down to Gordon. It emerged from the snow two or three feet below the crevasse. It was obvious what had happened: the rope had sliced through the lower side of the crevasse until its tangled mass had slammed up against the slot it had carved in the icy snow. By chance, Gordon had landed on a boulder embedded in the snow, and I made very sure that he got himself attached to that before I emerged from the safe haven of the crevasse.

If I hadn't gone into that lone micro-crevasse we would certainly have been killed one or two seconds later: the couloir curled off to the right, looking down, and had a very substantial rock wall on the far side. We would have slammed into that and been smashed to pieces long before we hit the screes several thousand feet below.

If we had become completely immobilized on the route, we would have had little chance of being rescued, because this was long before the days of mobile phones. And because of the midnight sun (dusk actually), we had brought no torches with us with which we could have flashed distress signals. In those days, there was certainly no helicopter rescue service in Romsdal, and I am not even sure there was a conventional mountain rescue team.

Once I was back in the lead, my memory of individual snow or rock pitches is much hazier than Gordon's. My entire focus was on the bigger picture. I realized that our getting up and off the mountain now depended on *me* not making any further screw-ups, especially with the route-finding.

I hauled Gordon by repetitively crouching down, taking in the rope as tight as possible, and then standing up, so as to pull him up mostly using my leg muscles. I did that for several thousand feet. Of course, Gordon in his damaged condition was taking much longer than usual to climb, even with this help. So I tried to use the time fruitfully by craning my upper body round as I was hauling, to plan the route ahead.

The hallucinations I had on the descent seemed very weird in retrospect, but not at the time. Unlike Gordon, I do not remember being shocked when perceived objects and people literally seemed to meld into rocks (or streaks on rocks), whereas Gordon seems to have been in a state of heightened awareness, probably brought on by the pain of his knee and the need to pick his way very carefully. By then I was too zombified to rationalize these illusions, and I did not say to myself: 'Er, John, you're hallucinating'. It was a bit like a popular interpretation of quantum physics: when a particle turns out to be a wave, or vice versa, so be it, it is not to be queried! By that stage, I was not frightened at all. I was just going through the process of self-rescue like an automaton – very far removed from consciously 'fighting for my life'.

The Norwegian driver who picked us up took one look at us and Gordon's football-sized, purple knee, and said, 'I will take you straight to the hospital'. But we immediately begged, 'No, no, what we need is food and drink, before anything else: please take us somewhere where we can eat.' He took some persuading that this was the correct order of priorities.

While we were being driven along in the car, we gave the driver a bare-bones description of our 56-hour epic. He brought us to the restaurant at Åndalsnes railway station, which in those days was a popular place for locals to meet for lunch. When we walked into the restaurant behind our Norwegian driver, Gordon was limping very slowly and got left far behind.

The room was pretty full, but everyone turned round and stared at us as though they had seen ghosts. Suddenly all eyes were on Gordon and the conversation stopped almost completely. Everyone was staring at him, as he was literally dragging his left leg along, with his eyes fixed straight ahead at the food counter.

The manager of the restaurant walked over to our rescuer, and there was a rapid exchange in Norwegian: our driver was obviously explaining how he had found us and how we had come to be in our present condition. Then the manager turned to me, and said percussively and with emphasis:

'Choose *anything* you like, it's on me!' I was taken aback by his immediate show of generosity.

When we got to the food counter, we found the servers' English wasn't very good, so we were simply pointing at the various samples behind the glass. 'We'll have one of those, and one of those … and one of those.' We ordered a quite ridiculous quantity. Six whole platefuls of the most wondrous looking stuff: steaks, seafood, you name it.

So we had ordered this huge amount of food, equivalent to about three meals each, including the very best thing: the ludicrously expensive sirloin steak. We both put the first morsels in our mouths, of some wonderful steak or something, and sat looking at each other for a few minutes while we just chewed and chewed, and tried to swallow … it tasted fantastically strong, very peculiar indeed … Our mouths stung as though we were trying to eat stinging nettles, and eventually we had no choice but to spit it out, into our hands, almost in unison. We just could not swallow it. We tried everything we'd got, with just the same result. Our throats just could not do it. All we found we could get down in the end was some soup. So once we'd got that down, we ordered some more, and had that too.

Eventually we were driven back to Fiva Farm. We thanked our driver profusely, assuring him that Gordon would go and see a doctor very soon. Gordon picked up a stick and we made our way slowly along the path towards our tent.

It was now a beautiful late afternoon, with everything in the Rauma valley bathed in a golden light … and in a line abreast coming towards us were four climbers: our companions Hugh and

Brian, and two others whom we didn't know … our rescue party on the way out to look for us and raise the alarm. And then we were all smiling and grinning from ear to ear, and back-slapping like Russian cosmonauts returning to the Cosmodrome having survived a *bad* landing. Then we all started going back to the tents.

The next two climbers we met on the path were Bill Lounds and Tony Charlton, who had been on the Troll Pillar opposite us during our ascent. Tony immediately said, in a flat Lancastrian tone:

'So you had an epic then?'

I was amazed that they knew about it.

'How did you know?'

'Well, you don't *look* too good!'

We threw down our gear, collapsed into our tent, and Hugh and Brian passed in mugs of hot chocolate. We were still not capable of getting down solids.

Brian told us they'd been really concerned when they'd arrived and found that we had still not got back over a day after we had said we would on our note. They attempted to organize a search party amongst the other British who'd also just arrived, but the trouble was they had only the vaguest idea of where we'd actually gone. The other climbers were pretty indifferent. Apparently one of them just said: 'Don't *worry* about it! If your friends come back, then that'll be *fine*; if they don't, then you won't have to bother!'

It was late afternoon when we crashed out, and we both slept for an unbroken twenty hours, the longest we'd ever slept in our lives. It was some time in the afternoon the next day when we awoke. Whilst we were asleep, Hugh and Brian had made an enormous meal, knowing we were absolutely starving, and as soon as we were out of the tent we gobbled that down. This time we managed to eat very successfully.

Suddenly Hugh said he could smell Gordon's knee:

'That's gangrene, that is. You need to get to a doctor as soon as possible.'

But by now it was too late for Gordon to get to see a doctor even that day. The transport from Fiva farm to Åndalsnes was awkward:

there was an evening 'milk bus', but it would get there too late.

It was late morning on the Thursday before Gordon got to see a doctor in Åndalsnes. The man spent an inordinate time prodding the knee painfully with needles, but failed to remove any of the fluid. Nevertheless, he pronounced it gangrenous, and said that Gordon must go immediately to Molde Hospital. That was about 70 miles away!

After a long journey by three separate ferries, Gordon arrived there about 10 p.m. There were X-rays and then a long wait before the surgeon reported that nothing was broken, but every tendon was torn and, because of the gangrene, everything now depended on penicillin. If that did not work, they would have no choice but to amputate the leg the very next day, because it would then be a question of the sooner the better.

The knee was operated on in the small hours of the morning, about a hundred hours after the accident. The doctors managed to extract all the fluid, and then injected a massive dose of penicillin under the kneecap (which was apparently absolute agony). Later, Gordon woke to find the knee had miraculously gone right back down to its normal size and looked like a shrivelled prune, a garish mixture of black, blue, and yellow. He was in a very small ward with about eight beds (with only a few occupied) and a panoramic window looking out over fjords. It was more like a luxury hotel than a hospital! The weather was now beautifully alpine, and the view across the fjord extended the whole way to a snowy-looking Store Trolltind, about seventy miles away.

Fortunately, this five-star treatment and hospitality cost nothing because Norway has had reciprocal health care with Britain since the Second World War, as a gesture of mutual respect for fighting the Nazis. (Of course, reciprocal, universal health care is now the norm with developed countries – with one notable exception!) The staff and nurses were very friendly, and Gordon was now feeling on top of the world, but *ravenously* hungry. However, that was soon cured, because it seemed that about every twenty minutes a food trolley was brought round, and he was able to stuff himself with superb open sandwiches. The surgeon was very happy when he came in to see him.

I also recovered very fast. The day after waking up, I had moved to the fully-appointed Åndalsnes campsite at Setnesmoen. I was on cloud nine; you can see how happy I am to be alive in this picture of me reclining beside our tent and battered-looking climbing gear.

Within a few days, I was climbing again on Bispen and Romsdalshorn with our other climbing companions. Gordon returned from the hospital a few days later, and we moved to the so-called 'British campsite', just a few hundred yards down the road from the Åndalsnes campsite where I was already established, right next to the Rauma River. It was by now occupied by many tents, and the list of climbers who'd congregated there was like a who's who of some of the biggest names in British climbing, including the very famous Joe Brown. He'd already heard about our epic and now wanted to climb the Fiva Route himself with Geoff Birtles, presumably as a warm-up and to reconnoiter the possibility of new routes on either side.

We were invited over to his big blue tent, but we were very shy because Joe was like a kind of demigod to us. It was a bit like being ushered into the presence of a sheik or something. Joe and Geoff gave us a brew, while asking us questions about the route. We warned them not to take any notice of the misleading cairn (as we then thought it was). I told them that the cairn was a 'complete red herring' and that they should 'avoid the main gully like the plague'. Gordon remembers cringing slightly because I was speaking to these down-to-earth, famous climbers in a very posh voice and using very posh expressions.

When Brown and Birtles returned a couple of days later, they pronounced it as being 'as serious as the North Face of the Eiger' in the current conditions. It had taken them eleven hours, even though they had soloed the whole thing – apart from the pitch we now refer to as the 'Brown-Birtles Crack', which was just above the point where I turned back in the left-hand gully. They told us it would have been Hard Very Severe or Extreme on English gritstone.

The Fiva Route has a unique character that reflects the cleverness of Arne Randers Heen who made the first ascent with his cousin Eirik in 1931. The correct route, which he got dead right on the first ascent, was rather brilliant in that it did not go up the most obvious line (the 'main gully' where we had our accident). Presumably he knew exactly how exposed to stone fall it would be, and that rotten snow was probably the norm there in summer. The line he took cleverly strung together a series of ribs and scarcely entered a single gully in well over seven thousand feet of climbing. This was the key piece of information that the guidebook failed to convey; in fact it implied the opposite: that most of the route was gully climbing.

Incidentally, the crux of the route for Heen was the steep slabby wall left of what he called 'the lid', and Gordon has called 'the coffin'. In an article about it in a Norwegian journal of 1932 (that we recently discovered), Eirik Heen wrote:

> Arne hadn't got far when the question of a runner occupied his thoughts. Soon the question became more intense, but I could offer no encouraging answer. After a while, he decided to continue thirty feet to a difficult block, which protruded from

the wall. This turned out to be loose and demanded the utmost care. There was 130 feet of useless rope between myself and Arne before he found any runners … The excitement here was possibly more than we had hoped for.'

When Eirik joined him, he found that Arne had had to belay on the loose block because he'd run out of rope. He continues:

> [My] excitement was certainly not reduced when I later released my belay and the whole block … fell off! Typical Troll Wall!

This is the very same place where Gordon had the most trouble seconding me with his damaged knee, and the point where Tom Patey failed on a winter attempt in 1960.

Although the Heens got the ascent line dead right, they made the same route-finding error as us on the descent. When they found their way blocked by the slabs, they climbed back up a long way, like ourselves, and got benighted.

> It rained and snowed, so it was not particularly pleasant lying there, soaked to the skin and freezing cold, with no food, sucking on wet moss for water …

In the early morning they came down by a different line, somehow avoiding the slabs completely, and by the time they reached the road they were really motoring: they 'walked' the last ten kilometers home in one hour, or so Eirik claimed! But they were legendarily fit, and Arne Randers Heen became synonymous with the climbing history of Romsdal for nearly forty years, culminating with his stupendous first ascent of the Troll Pillar with Ralph Hoibakk in 1958, which at the time was certainly one of the longest and best rock climbs in the world. (With 11,500 feet of climbing, it is still Europe's longest rock climb.)

Arne's reputation for boldness was typified by his penchant for making enormous leaps between pinnacles near the tops of mountains – there is a very famous one that he did between the 'horns' of the Svolvaer Goat in Lofoten. And in their account of the first ascent of the Fiva route, there is a photograph showing Arne making an enormous unroped leap across a gap at the top of the Trolltind wall, which Gordon and I have identified as the notch of Brur Skar. (We went back there in the summer of 2009 – because it was exactly forty years after our epic – and found Brur Skar to be at least as dramatic and gripping a viewpoint as we remembered.) Amazingly, the line of Heen's jump almost certainly took him right out over the abyss. The old photograph of the leaping Heen also shows him grasping a strange piece of equipment to take on a rock leap: an ice axe. The leap was a long one that probably needed an aggressive run-up along the edge of the cliff itself. Is it possible that the ice axe was a safety aid of last resort should the jump fall short? – a device to catch the rock lip on the far side, and *perhaps* save him from making the vertical death-plunge of thousands of feet?

Heen was also a war hero, a central figure in the resistance movement against the Nazis for the whole of this region of Norway. Because the port of Åndalsnes was a potential landing place for the British, the Germans flattened the entire town one night, except for the railway station. Unlike Guernica, not a single inhabitant died, thanks to the very effective intelligence of the Norwegian underground: the whole town managed to evacuate before the bombing started. Heen also flew the Norwegian flag from the top of the Romsdalshorn (which incidentally he climbed 233 times in his lifetime), in defiance of the German occupiers who had banned the national flag.

Gordon's knee recovered very rapidly after our Fiva misadventure (though it was still painful at times for a decade or more), which meant that, astonishingly, we were climbing together again about a fortnight later. We chose a pleasant Grade III route on the East Face of Bispen. The weather was good and Gordon's knee, though still a bit painful, stood up to the stresses well. I led the whole thing. I wrote in my diary: 'Very fast. Up and down to Stegfoss in four hours. Gordon's first climb in about two weeks'. The next day we decided to treat ourselves to a meal at Åndalsnes railway station to celebrate our survival again, and the rapid recovery of Gordon's knee.

As we walked up to the door of the restaurant, we noticed a white newspaper billboard nearby, on which was handwritten, in black capital letters, in English:

> 'ONE SMALL STEP FOR MAN,
> ONE GIANT LEAP FOR MANKIND'
> – NEIL ARMSTRONG

Although we hadn't heard about Apollo for several days, we understood immediately what this must mean. We also chortled for a second or two because of our own *unscheduled* giant leap a couple of weeks earlier.

We went into the restaurant and sat down, having decided to have waitress service, and spent quite a long time looking at the menu, and oddly no one seemed to be coming to serve us. Then suddenly a waitress appeared and plonked two huge meals down in front of us: the very best sirloin steaks you could possibly imagine – huge helpings with an enormous amount of vegetables and mushrooms and God knows what else.

'*No,*' we said, 'this is not for us; we haven't even ordered anything yet!'

'It is for *you*. It's from *us* – the manager has told us to give it to you, with the compliments of the restaurant.'

The manager had remembered the terrible state we'd been in when we went there before and how we'd been unable to eat anything. One remembers such kindnesses and generosities for the rest of one's life.

To cap off our holiday we climbed the West Ridge of Vengetind. We planned everything down to the minutest detail, and the climb went absolutely like clockwork. The rock was much lighter in colour than we had seen elsewhere in Romsdal, and generally of much better quality, making the climbing most enjoyable. We were back now to doing alternate leads, and it was incredible that Gordon was able to climb the route in this style – given that he had nearly had his leg amputated only a couple of weeks before. He says that, actually, his knee was still hurting quite a bit, and very tender, and that is the reason he is not standing in his photograph on the summit. Those summit photographs show us wearing exactly the same gear that we had on the Fiva route. They also show just how much ground we had covered in the few weeks since being photographed on our parents' lawn in England.

The Fiva epic did not put us off climbing. On our return, we went off to different universities, Gordon to Cardiff and I to Leeds. I picked Leeds not only because it had the course I wanted to study, but because it looked on the map as though it would make a good base for climbing. When I got there, I found that it had indeed got one of the most active climbing clubs in the UK, with a new generation of very keen and gifted climbers such as John Syrett, who became like a surrogate brother to me for several years. Climbing took such a hold on me that, after a year, I dropped out of my course and considered becoming a full-time climber. I spent much of 1971 climbing almost every day, and writing a climbing guide, before going to the Alps. But, after a successful but rather epic ascent of the Bonatti Pillar with members of the University club, my climbing fanaticism faded forever, and I realized there were other things to do in life. Gordon did a philosophy degree and went into the film industry, whereas I read geology and have been traveling the world in that profession ever since. However, Gordon and I have continued climbing and mountaineering at an intermediate level for over forty years.

What has climbing taught us? Mainly, that with focus and determination it is amazing what one can achieve in anything in any aspect of life in which one has a modicum of talent. And the Fiva experience itself? We regard it as an extraordinary privilege to have survived such a near-death experience, so that the rest of our lives has felt like one big bonus. We hardly ever let on about it – it is like our own very personal secret – but it has somehow informed everything that we do.

SOME
HISTORICAL
RELICS

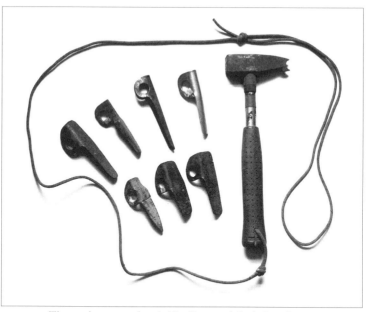

The actual pegs we used on the Fiva Route, and Gordon's peg hammer

Some of the nuts and krabs we used

John's ice hammer and Gordon's ice axe, rusted with age.
Neither of us ever used them again after the Fiva epic

The Troll Wall and the line of the Fiva Route (just right of centre) a week after our epic, now nearly completely free of snow.

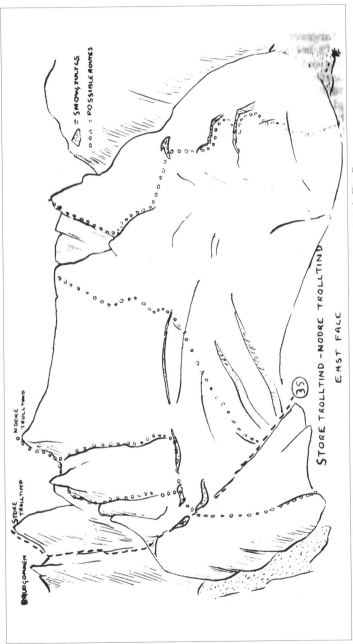

Above, and pp.204-5: three pages from the 1966 guidebook describing (35) the Fiva Route

Storgravfjell. After passing tarns, bear
left below Stabben and continue horizontally on
the cairned path below broken rocks of the
South West Face of Trollryggen and Trollkjeringa,
to Brur Skar. Continue past Brudgommen and Ugla
pinnacles, up a gully and across Ugla Skar by a
hole in the ridge. Follow the ridge to the top,
keeping to the left. (3 hrs.) Grade I.

There are also a number of other routes from
the North, mostly starting from Sogge, and the
peak has been climbed in winter. Its North Face
is reported to be unclimbed and is about 500ft.

35. <u>The East Face</u> Fiva Route (A.R.Heene and
E. Heene 1931)

A tedious introduction, mostly on grass, with
some climbing in the upper half. Nevertheless,
some splendid mountain scenery and good views of
the Trolltind Wall which is immediately opposite.
If there is a lot of snow present, there is some
danger of avalanches. Well over 6,000 feet of
climbing. Grade IV inf.

An obvious rake slants diagonally across the
East Face from right to left, finishing in the
prominent gully below the South East Face of Store
Trolltind. This is followed up interminable grass
ledges to the snow patch at the foot of the gully.
Continue up the small left gully or its left wall
(dependent on conditions) for several hundred
feet, passing difficulties on the left till a
steep crag is reached. Pass below this moving
right into the main gully and escaping by a hole
and chimney to Ugla Skar. The Ordinary Route
is then followed to the summit. (8-12 hrs.)

This route was attempted in winter by Tom
Patey and party who reached a point below the
ridge in one day, but unable to find the hole, they
were forced to retreat. It was also attempted
in winter 1966 by a Norwegian and two Swedes, and
all were tragically killed by an avalanche when
half way up the face on their fourth day.

√ 36. <u>Descent</u> is by the Ordinary Route, or - more
interesting - by the West Ridge and the pinnacles
of Trollklorne, to Sogge. (Either way 3 hrs.)

NODRE TROLLTIND
(1,618 m = 5,330 ft.)

37. <u>The North Ridge</u> Ordinary Route (W. Bromley-
Davenport M.P. and J. Venge 1870)

An easy scramble from Sogge, across Norafjell
and up the ridge. Grade 1 (4 hrs.)

The East Face of this peak is a tremendous
expanse of rock curving up from glaciated slabs
to a steep wall, and about 5,000 feet high. It
presents numerous possibilities for routes, some
of which finish on the smaller summits to its
North.   *Climbed Hull University Party, 1966*

38. <u>Descent</u> is by the ordinary route (2 hrs.)

MILLARMITT
'RAINSTORMPROOF'

half-finger Climbers' Mitt
with unique Slip-resisting Palm
19/- pair + 9d post.

as supplied to
Rimmon Trolltind   **The**
Expedition - 1965 **Climbers   Shop**
COMPSTON CORNER
AMBLESIDE, WESTMORLAND.

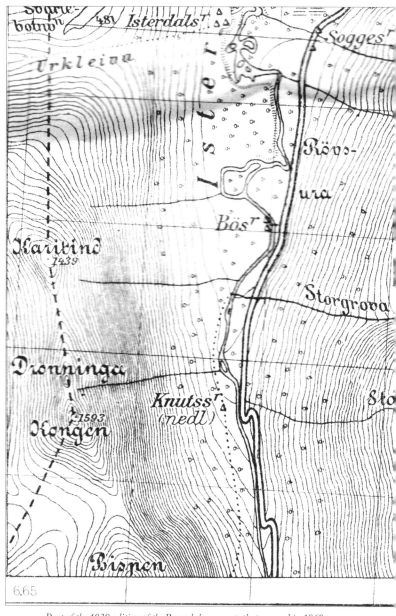

Part of the 1939 edition of the Romsdal area map that we used in 1969.
Above: Isterdal. The reason we couldn't find Stegfoss is that it's off the bottom of the map.

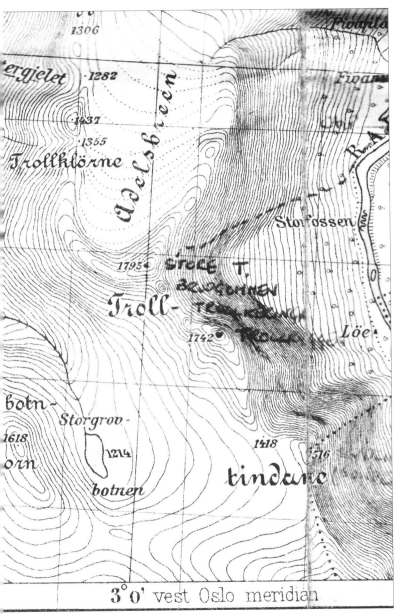

Above: Store Trolltind and the Troll Wall with Romsdal to its right (east).
In biro we had inked in the line of the Fiva Route, from Fiva Farm, top right

Gordon's main waistline karabiner – a Hiatt 'D-screw' – that he used on the Fiva Route to attach himself to the climbing ropes, now badly rusted after years in a cellar. This kind of heavy steel krab was rendered obsolete by the advent of much lighter alloy designs in about 1970-71.

GLOSSARY OF CLIMBING TERMS

BELAY n. The means by which a climber attaches him/herself to a mountain/crag. v. 1. The process of attaching oneself to a mountain/crag. 2. Safeguarding the *leader* or the *second* by paying out or taking in the rope in the correct manner.

BIVVY A bivouac, or very rudimentary overnight camp on a mountain using minimal gear, often enforced by emergency.

KRAB = Karabiner. A metal snaplink used for *belaying* or for *runners*.

LEADER The climber who leads a *pitch* on a climb.

NUT A piece of metal, typically a small wedge, attached to a sling and *krab* to make a *runner*

PEG A piece of metal of various shapes and sizes (typically a knife-like blade) that can be driven into cracks in the rock with a peg hammer to make a *belay* anchor or a *runner*. It has an eyelet that enables the climbing rope to be clipped into it with a *krab*.

PITCH A section of a climb, usually comfortably shorter than the length of rope the climbers are using. At the top of each *pitch* the *leader* will rig up a new *belay*.

PROTECTION = *runners*

RUNNER = 'running belay'. The means by which a *leader* protects himself by clipping the rope behind him into *krabs* that are attached to the rock by *nuts* or *pegs*, to reduce the length of any fall. The rope runs through the *krabs* behind the *leader* as he/she climbs.

SECOND A climber who follows the *leader* up a *pitch* with the safety ('protection') of the rope from above.

VS Very Severe. A classic grade for a difficult rock climb in the UK, now rather moderate by modern standards.

FURTHER READING

Tony Howard, *Climbs, Scrambles and Walks in Romsdal*, revised 4th edition. Cordee, 2005

Tony Howard, *Troll Wall.* Vertebrate Publishing, 2011

For more useful information see:
www.nomadstravel.co.uk
and
www.romsdalsalpene.com

For further picture galleries and background information about this book see:
www.goldenarrowbooks.co.uk/fiva